OXFORD
SLAVONIC PAPERS

Edited by

I. P. FOOTE   G. S. SMITH

and

G. C. STONE

General Editor

NEW SERIES

VOLUME XXIII

OXFORD

AT THE CLARENDON PRESS

1990

Oxford University Press, Walton Street, Oxford OX2 6DP
Oxford New York Toronto
Delhi Bombay Calcutta Madras Karachi
Petaling Jaya Singapore Hong Kong Tokyo
Nairobi Dar es Salaam Cape Town
Melbourne Auckland
and associated companies in
Berlin Ibadan

Oxford is a trade mark of Oxford University Press

Published in the United States
by Oxford University Press, New York

© Oxford University Press 1990

British Library Cataloguing in Publication Data
Oxford Slavonic Papers: new series.
Vol. 23
1. Eastern Europe
I. Foote, I. P. (Irwin Paul), 1926–
II. Smith, G. S.   III. Stone, G. C.
947.0008
ISBN 0–19–815167–5

Library of Congress Cataloging in Publication Data
Data available

Typeset by Joshua Associates Ltd., Oxford
Printed in Great Britain
by Bookcraft (Bath) Ltd.
Midsomer Norton, Avon

THE editorial policy of the New Series of *Oxford Slavonic Papers* in general follows that of the original series, thirteen volumes of which appeared between the years 1950 and 1967. It is devoted to the publication of original contributions and documents relating to the languages, literatures, culture, and history of Russia and the other Slavonic countries, and appears annually. Reviews of individual books are not normally included, but bibliographical and review articles are published from time to time.

The British System of Cyrillic transliteration (British Standard 2979: 1958) has been adopted, omitting diacritics and using -y to express -й, -ий, -iй, and -ый at the end of proper names, e.g. Sergey, Dostoevsky, Bely, Grozny. For philological work the International System (ISO R/9) is used.

Editorial correspondence and typescripts should be addressed to Dr G. C. Stone at Hertford College, Oxford. Copies of the rules for style and presentation of typescripts will be supplied on request.

I. P. FOOTE
G. S. SMITH
G. C. STONE

Hertford College, Oxford

CONTENTS

A Stemma for the First Letter of A. M. Kurbsky

By DONALD OSTROWSKI

IN 1971 Edward L. Keenen, on the basis of twelve copies known to him, published the first stemma (relationship of copies) of the first redaction of Kurbsky's First Letter (hereafter KI[a]) (see Fig. 1).[1] In 1976 A. A. Zimin investigated more manuscript copies (nineteen in all) and provided a different stemma for the Letter (see Fig. 2).[2] In 1979 Ya. S. Lur'e and Yu. D. Rykov included more manuscript copies (making twenty-four in all) and provided two alternative stemmata for KI[a], the second of which was based on Zimin's stemma (see Figs. 3 and 4).[3] They did not, however, discuss the advantages of one over the other or even say why they had provided two alternative stemmata.

In 1987 B. N. Morozov published a previously unknown copy of KI[a].[4] For the purposes of the following discussion I shall call this copy *T* and use the conventions adopted by Lur'e and Rykov (see Appendix) to designate the other manuscripts. Except for *Ов* and *T* I have had to rely on the critical apparatus provided by Lur'e and Rykov.[5] Where possible I have cross-checked the readings they give against those provided by Keenan. The difficulty of establishing a true stemma for KI[a] is increased by the following somewhat cryptic warning in Lur'e and Rykov's book:

In the publication of the Correspondence [. . .] we do not provide variants according to all copies of the letters. However, we do not limit ourselves only to the correction of clearly mistaken readings of the basic copies according to other copies of those same

---

[1] Edward L. Keenan, *The Kurbskii–Groznyi Apocrypha: The Seventeenth-Century Genesis of the 'Correspondence' Attributed to Prince A. M. Kurbskii and Tsar Ivan IV* (Cambridge, Mass., 1971), 14, 154. Keenan's stemma also includes four copies of the second redaction.

[2] A. A. Zimin, 'Pervoe poslanie Kurbskogo Ivanu Groznomu (tekstologicheskie problemy)', *Trudy Otdela drevnerusskoi literatury*, xxxi (1976), 200.

[3] *Perepiska Ivana Groznogo s Andreem Kurbskim*, ed. Ya. S. Lur'e and Yu. D. Rykov (L., 1979), 269, 270. See the Appendix to the present article for a table of the conventions adopted by Keenan, Zimin, and Lur'e and Rykov to designate the various manuscripts.

[4] B. N. Morozov, 'Pervoe poslanie Kurbskogo Ivanu Groznomu v sbornike kontsa XVI–nachala XVII v.', *Arkheograficheskii ezhegodnik za 1986 god* (M., 1987), 277–89.

[5] In 1975 I found in Moscow and included in my doctoral dissertation the text of a previously unknown copy of KI[a]. Donald Ostrowski, 'A "Fontological" Investigation of the Moscow Church Council of 1503' (unpublished Ph.D. dissertation, Ann Arbor, Michigan, 1977), 611–13. This copy (ГБЛ, Овчинников № 285) was subsequently designated *Ов* by Lur'e and Rykov.

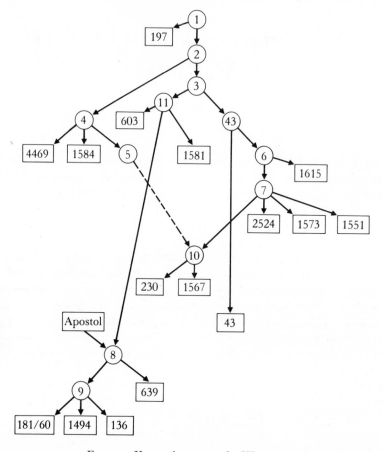

FIG. 1. Keenan's stemma for KI[a] (1971)

groups and types (видов), but we also provide variants that are characteristic for entire groups of copies.[6]

Since what constitutes a variant that is 'characteristic for entire groups of copies' is a matter of opinion and since it is not clear that they provide *all* variants even for those copies for which they do provide at least *some* variants, much of what I say here may have to be checked against the manuscripts. I have listed at the end of this article four significant places where Keenan's variants and those of Lur'e and Rykov for the copies of KI[a] do not agree.

My analysis of the relationship of copies of KI[a], based on the published text and variants provided by Lur'e and Rykov, has led me to the conclusion that their two stemmata (and that of Zimin) are insuffi-

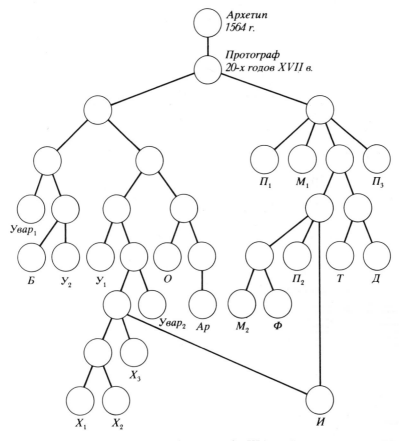

Архетип
1564 г.

Протограф
20-х годов XVII в.

$П_1$ M_1 $П_3$

$Увар_1$

$Б$ $У_2$ $У_1$ O $П_2$ T $Д$

$Увар_2$ Ap M_2 $Ф$

X_3

X_1 X_2 $И$

FIG. 2. Zimin's stemma for KI[a] (1976)

cient for a number of reasons. First, they are too 'neat'. All the extant copies derive directly from non-extant or hypothetical copies. In other words, no extant copy served as an exemplar for any other extant copy. Since we have twenty-five copies for a period of seventy years (1630–1700) (one copy, on average, for every 2.8 years) and since we have eleven copies from the 1630s alone (one copy, on average, for every year), it is odd that *all* intermediate copies have been destroyed.

Secondly, their stemmata have too little confluence, if one considers the varied nature of the readings. They show only one example of confluence, namely *Пн*, and this is presumably based only on the fact that where влас (the reading of first-group copies) appears in the text of *Пн* the scribe wrote власти (the reading of second-group copies) in the margin (variant 6ᵍп). The single instance of confluence then leaves unexplained how, for example, *Хл* (a first-group copy) picks up the

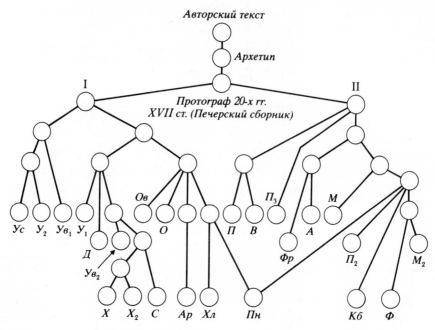

FIG. 3. Lur'e and Rykov's stemma (Variant 1) for KI[a] (1979)

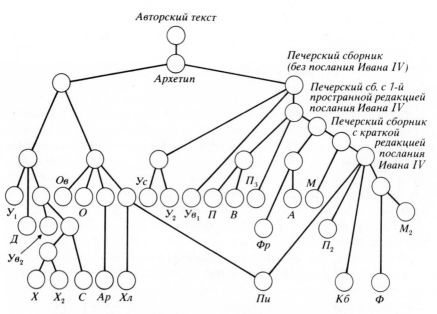

FIG. 4. Lur'e and Rykov's stemma (Variant 2) for KI[a] (1979)

readings of some copies of the second group, such as the ты in variant 6ᵍд–е, the согрешивша in variant 6ᵛр, the един of variant 7ᵛа–б, and how both *Хл* and *Ap* pick up the и in variant 8ʳр (although this may be a scribal accidental) and the в in variant 9ʳа (which is less likely to be an accidental). Also, it seems likely that *Хл* and *Ap* pick up their forms of у тебя (*Хл*: тебе) быти таковым потаковником (*Хл*: потаковщиком) from the second-group copies, while first-group copies have таким/ таким почитати (variant 8ᵛп–п). Is it likely, if у тебя быти таковым потаковником had been in the archetype, that it would have been shortened in almost identical ways at the common exemplar of *УсУв₁ У₂* (I am postulating what *У₂* would have had, had its text continued) and at the common exemplar of *У₁ ДУв₂ ХХ₂ С*, but not at the common exemplar of *ОвОАрХл*? Nor is it likely that the scribes of *Ap* and *Хл* came independently to the reading of the second group. Keenan has different views concerning the disposition of *Ap*, but I think those readings of *Ap* that do not agree with the *ООв* line can be ascribed to confluence with an *АФр*-type copy.

Thirdly, the relationship of the copies that Lur'e and Rykov give simply does not explain the readings that show up in the copies. They seem to depend too much on scribal coincidentals, that is, on two or more scribes coming up with the same reading independently. For example, in variant 7ᵛж, Lur'e and Rykov report that both *МФрАП₃* and *ОХл* omit мню. All the other cases have мню (or some form of it—*Ф*: мене, *Ap*: мне). If we accept the point that мню, as an interjection, is easily dropped, then its omission may be explained as a scribal accidental. But it is highly unlikely that a scribe would have restored it spontaneously. When we examine Lur'e and Rykov's stemmata, we find that *ПВП₃* derive from a shared exemplar. That is acceptable because we can postulate that мню is in their exemplar, which shows up also in *ПВ* and is omitted in *П₃*. But it is also omitted in *ФрА*, which share an exemplar. Therefore, it is likely that мню was omitted in their exemplar. However, мню still lives because the grandparent exemplar of *ФрА* feeds into the main line of the rest of second-group copies where that line shares an exemplar with the exemplar of *M*. Thus far, мню has been omitted independently by two scribes, namely that of *П₃* and that of the exemplar of *ФрА* (not to mention *О* and *Хл*). But now we have a third (or fourth or fifth) scribe omitting it. We are forced to the conclusion that мню must have been omitted in the main-line exemplar of *ФрАМ*. But, as we see, мню shows up again in *П₂ КбФМ₂*, all of which share a common exemplar with each other and through it with *ФрАМ*. Since it is unlikely that мню was added in their common exemplar (which, incidentally, is also attested by *Пн*) and since it is unlikely that it was omitted by half a dozen scribes independently, we can only conclude that something is awry. It would be possible to quote many further examples.

Fourthly and most importantly, Lur'e, Rykov, and Zimin make almost no value judgements concerning the differences between the first and second groups. They give the following variants as distinguishing the first group from the second: о сем глаголати/глаголати о всем (5^vа–а); $\varnothing$/о царю (5^vг–д); Про что/По что (5^vд–е); влас/власти (6^rп); силы/$\varnothing$ (6^rу); and the above-mentioned таким/у тебя быти таковым потаковником (8^vп–п). But which are preferable? Which are more likely to have been in the archetype?

My stemma (Fig. 5) represents the relationship of the copies (according to the readings presented in Lur'e and Rykov's critical apparatus) better than either of the Lur'e and Rykov stemmata, but I readily admit that it does not solve all the problems I have just pointed out. Clearly, Lur'e and Rykov are faced with a problem in placing $Ус У_2$ $Ув_1$. But their Variant 2 is closer to my proposal. It seems to me that first-group copies, especially $Ус У_2$ $Ув_1$ $ООвТ$, and to a lesser extent $У_1$ $Ув_2$, provide more or less direct information about the archetype, while second-group copies are derived from the first group. As for the significant variants given by Lur'e and Rykov, four (о сем глаголати/глаголати о всем; Про что/По что; влас/власти; and силы/$\varnothing$) are stand-offs as to which member of the pair is primary. And Про что/По что is not even a reliable determiner because four copies of the first group ($Ув_2$ $ОвАрХл$) share the По что of the second. However, two of their determiners ($\varnothing$/о царю and таким/у тебя . . .), plus three others that I have chosen (бысть/быста/быша (6^rв); Он Бог есть/Он бо есть/Он бо весть/etc. (7^vв–г); and безгласным/бесовския согласным/бесом согласным (8^rк–л)), suggest a clear direction of primacy. These five cruces are significant enough to sway all the other stand-offs in one direction.

1. $\varnothing$/о царю. In connection with this determiner we should also take into consideration the presence or absence of ти. There are thus four groups of copies: (i) those with neither ти nor о царю ($ДООвХлАр$); (ii) those with ти but not о царю ($Ув_1$ $Ус У_2$ $У_1$ $Ув_2$ $ХХ_2$ $СТ$); (iii) those with о царю but not ти ($ММ_2$ $П_2$ $ФК6АП_3$ $Пн$); and (iv) those with both ти and о царю ($ПВФр$). If ти, о царю is primary, as Lur'e and Rykov believe, then how can we explain the omission of ти in some cases, of о царю in other cases, and of both ти and о царю in still others? It is more likely that the phrase ти, о царю represents the combination of two branches, the ти branch and the о царю branch. The $\varnothing$ branch probably developed from the ти branch because a scribe, failing to perceive ти as the short-form dative, interpreted изрещити as an incorrect infinitive form and substituted изрещи. This misunderstanding may have resulted from the fact that ти is in an odd position here. The question arises whether о царю represents a replacement for ти or a filling-in of a blank space. Since there does not appear to be any reason

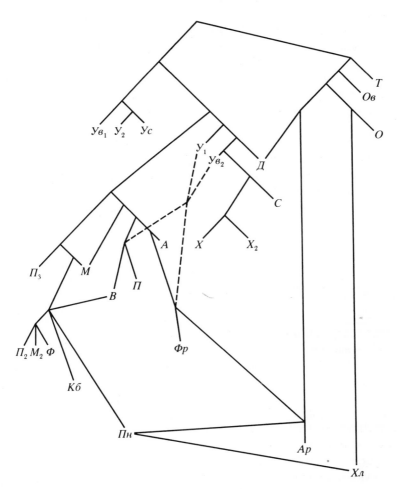

Fɪɢ. 5. Proposed stemma for KIᵃ

why a scribe should feel the absence of ти to be an omission (and because of other considerations of the copies involved), it seems more likely that о царю replaced ти in an attempt to harmonize with the царю of the first line and of the next line. Seventeenth-century style did not demand the alteration of forms to prevent repetition. In my stemma the combination of ти with о царю occurs twice: once at the common exemplar of *ПВ* and once at the combination of *Фр* with the *У₁ Ув₂* hypothetical copy (see below). Therefore, the copies *Ув₁ УсУ₂ У₁ Ув₂ ХХ₂ СТ* carry the primary reading.

2. бысть/быста/быша. Here быша seems to be correct (if, as we suspect, its subject was plural, i.e. many German towns). But it occurs

in scattered manuscripts, namely *ФрУв₂ ХлОТ*. It is possible that
бысть is to be interpreted as бысте (3rd person dual, Church Slavonic).
In Old Russian the equivalent form is быста. But it is not clear why
plural быша should have been changed to dual. However, if бысть was
the primary reading, the change бысть → быста/бысте is understand-
able. The dual form involves changing only one letter. Some scribes,
moreover, were capable of deducing the correct form. This would
account for the fact that быша is scattered, it having been independently arrived at as the correct form. Therefore, *Ув₁ УсУ₂ У₁ ПнХХ₂
СОвД* carry the primary reading.

3. Он Бог есть/Он бо есть/Он бо весть/etc. I postulate Бог весть as
a secondary harmonization with the end of the previous sentence. It is
also easier to explain б̄гесть → боесть as a case of a splotched г in the
manuscript being interpreted as an o (rather than of a splotched o
being interpreted as a г). Therefore, I assume this progression:

$$
\text{Он Бог есть}
\begin{cases}
\rightarrow \text{Он бо весть}
\begin{cases}
\rightarrow \text{Он Бог весть} \\
\rightarrow \text{Он бо Бог весть}
\end{cases} \\
\rightarrow \text{Он бо есть} \quad\quad \rightarrow \text{Он бо Бог есть} \\
\rightarrow \varnothing
\end{cases}
$$

The primary reading is carried by *ВУв₁ УсУ₂*.

4. безгласным/бесовския согласным/бесом согласным. It seems
most likely that безгласным was the original reading. That explains its
presence in the early copies of the two main branches in my stemma,
that is, *Ув₁ У₂ О*. The problem is that the boyars are not silent, because
the text has just said that they are flatterers. Here безгласные may
mean that they are held back by fear from saying what they think. But
scribes seem to have felt uneasy with that word. Therefore, the scribe of
Ус added a syllable to make безсогласным, but this conflicts with the
согласующим just preceding. Therefore, a different 'improvement' was
made in the exemplar of *У₁*, by the creation of a demonic table
(бесовския трапезы согласным). This was passed on, in my stemma,
to second-group copies as трапезы бесовские согласным and to
Д Ув₂ ХХ₂ С as agreeing-with-the devil boyars (бесом согласным). The
picking-up by *Фр* of the reading бесовския трапезы согласным (= *У₁*)
suggests to me a more direct connection between *Фр* and *У₁* (see
below). The reading of *Ар* (бесовския трапезы твоим) I take to come
from the dropping of согласным after трапезы and to represent the
У₁ → *Фр* connection. Finally, the readings of *Хл* and *ПнТ* (бесо-
гласной/бесогласным) I once thought might represent a direct connection with *Ус* (безсогласным). But the spelling suggests a much simpler
explanation, namely parablebsis: бесо[вские со]гласным → бесогласным. The primary reading is carried by *Ув₁ У₂ О*.

5. таким/у тебя быти таковым потаковником. The shorter reading

(таким) should be accepted as primary. Two attempts were made to build it up: (i) таким почитати ($У_1$ $Ув_2$ XX_2 C ($Д$: таких почитати)) and (ii) у тебя быти таким потаковником ($МП_3$ $П_2$ M_2 $ФПн$)/у тебя быти таковым потаковником ($ПВАФрАр$). The reading of T ([. . .]такати) may again be the result of parablepsis, that is: так[им почит]ати → такати. The потаковщиком/потаковъщиком of $XлКб$ is most likely a coincidental agreement. Therefore, the primary reading is carried by $Ув_1$ $Ус$.

As a result of my analysis, I conclude that $Ув_1$ $УсУ_2$ seem to represent the archetype best. But some primary readings that do not appear in them do show up in $ООвУ_1$ $Ув_2$. I agree with Lur'e and Rykov in their stemmatic representation of the relationship of copies within each of the subgroups: $УсУ_2$ $Ув_1$; $У_1$ $Ув_2$ XX_2 C; $ООв$; and $КбМ_2$ $П_2$ $Ф$. However, it seems that, while $Д$ certainly derives from the $У_1$ $Ув_2$ line, it does share some readings with the $ООв$ line. Most notable is the heading:

$Ов$	$Д$
Послание князя Андрея Курбъскаго. Киязь Андрей Михайлович Курбской пишет царю государю и великому князю Ивану Васильевичю всеа Русии, изменив, в Литву отъехав.	Князь Андрей Михайлович Курпъской пишет царю государю и великому князю Ивану Васильевичю всеа Русии, изменив, в Литву отъехав.

There is also a similarity here with $У_1$ but the scribe of $Д$, working from $У_1$ alone, could not possibly have duplicated the exact wording of $Ов$, even by chance. Also, there are other similarities in $Д$ with the $ООв$ line in contradistinction to $У_1$ $Ув_2$. For example, in variant 5^{в}в: прегорчайшего ($Д$)/прегорчайшаго ($Ов$) vs. прегоршаго ($У_1$ $Ув_2$); in variant 5^{в}г–д: ∅ ($ДООв$) vs. ти ($У_1$ $Ув_2$); in variant 7^{г}г: труды и поты ($ДОв$) vs. труды, поты ($У_1$ $Ув_2$); in variant 7^{г}е–е: не познах ($ДООв$) vs. познах ($У_1$ $Ув_2$); in variant 7^{г}з: дальных ($ДОв$) vs. дальних ($У_1$ $Ув_2$); in variant 7^{в}а–б: лутчи ($ДО$) vs. лутче ($У_1$)/лучши ($Ув_2$); and in variant 8^{г}н: иже и з детьми ($ДО$) vs. иже детьми ($У_1$ $Ув_2$).

Basically, my thinking on the $П_3$ $МПВАП_2$ M_2 $ФКб$ intermezzo is this: (i) a revision of the text occurred in the hyparchetype; (ii) some copies maintain a more or less direct connection with the reading of that hyparchetype; (iii) contamination has occurred, but has not necessarily resulted in the restoration of omissions. To establish the relationship of these copies, I selected nine significant variants, which in the hyparchetype read: у тебя быти таким потаковником; Он Бог есть; языцех (5^{в}е); дальных окольных (or some variation using two words) (7^{г}з); согреших (6^{в}р); за тя (6^{в}л–л); на тя (6^{в}м–н); мню (7^{в}ж); and прегорчайшаго (5^{в}в).

$П_3$ and M must share an exemplar (which feeds into $П_2$ M_2 $Ф$ and which is not shared immediately by $\varPi$, B, or A) because of the reading у тебя быти таким потаковником and the absence of any form of Он Бог есть. $\varPi$ and B share an exemplar with $\varPi_2 M_2 \varPhi K б$ that is not shared by $\varPi_3$, M, or A because of the absence of языцех (5^{r}e) and the reading дальноконных (7^{r}з). $M\varPi B$ must also derive from an ancestor of A that is not shared by $\varPi_3$ or $\varPi_2 M_2 \varPhi K б$ because of the agreement of согрешивша (6^{v}р). But $\varPi$ and B share an exemplar with A that is not shared by $M\varPi_3 \varPi_2 M_2 \varPhi K б$ (and which leads to the hyparchetype) because of the reading прегорчайшаго/прегорчяйшего (5^{v}в) and because of the presence of some form of Он Бог есть. M shares an exemplar with $\varPi_2 M_2 \varPhi K б$ that is not shared with $\varPi_3$, $\varPi$, B, or A because of the omission of за тя (6^{v}л–л) and of на тя (6^{v}м–н). Finally, $MA\varPi_3$ share an exemplar against $\varPi B \varPi_2 M_2 \varPhi K б$ because of the omission of мню (7^{v}ж).

$\varPhi p$ and A have several discrete similarities: всевредно/всевредна (6^{r}г); умышляя (8^{r}д); ко гласом/ко гласующим (8^{r}з); Иродовых (8^{r}о); погубляти (8^{v}к); рожен бысть (8^{v}л–л); делом/не делом (8^{v}м); omission of до десяти родов (9^{r}б–б); and the addition of таковых (9^{r}г). Most of these agreements not shared with other copies occur near the end of the text. Earlier in the text, $\varPhi p$ picks up some readings from a copy that at times seems to agree with $У_1$ and at times with $У в_2$. Therefore, I postulate a hypothetical copy that combines their readings, which were then passed on to an exemplar of $\varPhi p$. For example, this hypothetical copy must have had ти (5^{v}г–д) from either $У_1$ or $У в_2$, быша (6^{r}в) from $У в_2$, неслышанныя (5^{v}к) from $У в_2$, and глаголет (6^{r}с) from $У_1$. This hypothetical copy may also have been the contaminator of $\varPi B$. For example, besides the ти in ти, о царю, $\varPi B$ may have taken седяше/сядеше (6^{r}т) (both $У_1$ and $У в_2$) and Кроновых (8^{r}о) (both $У_1$ and $У в_2$) from it rather than from the hyparchetype since none of $\varPi B$'s sister copies ($\varPi_3$, M, or A) has these readings. The postulation of two hypothetical copies, one based on $\varPi B$ and the other on $\varPhi p$, is unnecessary.

The final three copies ($A p \varPi н Х л$) all show evidence of confluence, that is, of uniting readings from the first and second groups. For example, all three have such readings that signal the first group as: о сем глаголати; силы; and губителя (8^{r}к). Also they have in common with the second group such readings as: у тебя быти таковым потаковником (or a variant); и (8^{r}р); and в (9^{r}а). Within the first group all three copies seem to derive from the $OO в$ line. For example, all three have Послание in their titles and some form of Он бо есть, which appears in O. But $A p$, on one hand, and $\varPi н Х л$, on the other, seem to derive from different lines of the second group. $A p$ seems to pick up readings that may have come from an $A \varPhi p$-type copy; for example: же и (5^{r}б); глаголеть (6^{r}с); вопия (7^{v}л); писанейцех сие (8^{r}т–у); хотяща

(8ᵛи); and рожден бысть (8ᵛл–л), besides the above-mentioned second-group readings. *Пн* seems to pick up readings from an M_2 $П_2$ *Ф*-type copy; for example: же (6ᵛв–в); 7072-го. Курбскаго ко государю (8ᵛз); and у тебя быти таким потаковником. But *Пн* seems to get its *ООв* line readings through a proximity with *Ap*; for example: лутче (7ᵛа–б); хотяща (8ᵛи); and рождьшия мя (7ᵍд–д). Finally, *Хл* seems to pick up readings directly from *Пн*. I conclude that *Хл* derives from *Пн* rather than that they share an exemplar owing to the progression: трапезы бесовские согласующим твоим ($П_2$ M_2 *Ф*) → трапезы бесогласным твоим (*Пн*) → трапезы бесогласной твоим (*Хл*). Other discrete, or semi-discrete, readings that they share are: a similarity in the heading; неслыхано (5ᵛк); их тебе (6ᵍа); уже не (6ᵍи); and Он бо есть Бог (7ᵛв–г). This relationship of *Пн* and *Хл*, however, does not explain why *Хл* picks up the таковым of *ПВАФрАр* instead of таким of *Пн*, and the потаковщиком of *Кб*. And *Хл* seems to have a closer affinity to an *О*-type copy than to the *ОвД* line because of the reading далних и окольних (7ᵍз) and the absence of мню (7ᵛж).

Keenan, on the one hand, and Lur'e and Rykov, on the other, differ in their presentation of the variants in at least four significant cases:

1. In variant 10 Keenan gives *Ap* as reading Но сего о сем вся пору не попустих глаголат, while in a subsequent unpublished article he gives the *Ap* reading as Но сего о сем вся порядy не попустих моему языку.[7] Lur'e and Rykov seem to give И больши сего о сем глаголати вся по ряду не попустих моему языку (5ᵛа–а, б).

2. In variant 79 Keenen has $П_2$: подвигл; and *О*: подвигнул with the implication that the other manuscripts read воздвигл as in his text. But Lur'e and Rykov have *Фр*: возвел; *О*: подвигнул; and *ОвАр*: воздвигл with the implication that all the rest read подвигл as in their text (6ᵛб).

3. In variant 80 Keenan has *Ус*: лжени и; and $П_2$: же with the rest as лжей и. Lur'e and Rykov agree with Keenan as far as *Ус* and $П_2$ are concerned, but, of the variants Keenan reports, they have $П_3$: лжей; and M_2 *О*: же (6ᵛв–в).

4. Finally, and most importantly, Keenan gives in variant 93 *О*: за благая моя воздал ми вси злая. Lur'e and Rykov give a different word order for *О*: воздал ми еси злая за благая (6ᵛи–и, к), but there remains the question whether they have inadvertently dropped the моя from *О*.

---

[7] Edward Keenan, 'Eshche raz o "Perepiske" Groznogo s Kurbskim' (typescript).

APPENDIX

Correlation Table of Designations of Manuscript Copies

Manuscript copy	Keenan (1971)	Zimin (1976)	Lur'e/Rykov (1979)
First group			
ГБЛ, собр. Овчинникова, № 285	—	—	$Ов$
ГБЛ, собр. Ундольского, № 603	603	$У_1$	$У_1$
ГБЛ, собр. Ундольского, № 720	—	$У_2$	$У_2$
ГИМ, собр. Уварова, № 168 (1584)	1584	$Увар_1$	$Ув_1$
ГБЛ, собр. ОИДР, № 197	197	$О$	$О$
ГБЛ, собр. Усова, № 69 (Муз. № 4469)	4469	$Б$	$Ус$
ЦГАДА, МГА МИД (ф. 181) оп. 1, № 461/929	—	—	$Д$
ГИМ, собр. Уварова, № 330 (1581)	1581	$Увар_2$	$Ув_2$
ГПБ, Основное собр., F.IV.165 (Толстой № 64)	—	$Х_1$	$Х$
ГПБ, Основное собр., F.IV.598	—	$Х_2$	$Х_2$
ГПБ, собр. СПб. духовной академии, А 1/91	—	$Х_3$	$С$
ГПБ, собр. Русского Археолог. общества, № 43	43	$Ар$	$Ар$
ГИМ, собр. А. И. Хлудова, № 246	—	—	$Хл$
ИРЛИ, собр. Пинежское, № 112	—	$И$	$Пн$
ГПБ, Основное собр., Q.XVII.67 (Толстой № 195)	—	—	
Second group			
ЦГВИА, ф. Военно-ученого архива, № 3, ч. 1	—	—	$В$
ГПБ, собр. М. П. Погодина, № 1567	1567	$П_1$	$П$
ГИМ, Музейское собр., № 1551	1551	$М_1$	$М$
ГПБ, собр. М. П. Погодина, № 1615	1615	$П_3$	$П_3$
БАН, собр. Текущих поступлений, № 230	230	$А$	$А$
ГИМ, Музейское собр., № 2524	2524	$М_2$	$М_2$
ГПБ, собр. М. П. Погодина, № 1573·	1573	$П_2$	$П_2$
ГПБ, Основное собр., F.XVII.15	—	$Т$	$Фр$
ГБЛ, собр. И. М. Фадеева, № 62	—	$Ф$	$Ф$
ЦГАДА, МГА МИД (ф. 181), № 352/801	—	—	$Кб$

'The Lawes of Russia Written':
An English Manuscript on Muscovy
at the End of the Sixteenth Century

By MARIA SALOMON AREL

THE Rare Book Department of the McLennan Library at McGill University, Montreal, is the present repository of an English manuscript (shelf-mark MS 477) of potentially great interest to historians of Russia, especially of the Muscovite period. It was purchased by Professor Philip Longworth from Maggs Brothers of London in 1980 and later donated to McGill University.[1] It is neither signed nor dated and is divided into three sections. The first section provides an English translation of the 1550 *Sudebnik*, the second consists of a description of the Muscovite social and administrative hierarchy, and the third contains an outline of the Muscovite bureaucratic apparatus. This article sets out to describe the manuscript, discuss the possible date of its composition and the question of its authorship, to publish the text of the last two sections, and to assess their value as a source for the history of Muscovy. The first section (the translation of the *Sudebnik*) is not dealt with here, as it appears to merit separate treatment.[2]

[1] This article is based on a thesis entitled 'An Edition and Analysis of the "Lawes of Russia" Manuscript, with Particular Reference to the Bureaucratic Apparatus of the Muscovite State', which was approved for the degree of MA in the Department of History, McGill University, Montreal, in 1988. I take this opportunity to thank Professor Philip Longworth for placing the manuscript at my disposal and for the constructive criticism to which he subjected my project at every stage. Dr G. C.Stone, Mr J. S. G. Simmons, Professor Geraldine Phipps, and Professor Samuel Baron all discussed a number of troublesome points and queries with me. Special thanks are due to the Social Science and Humanities Research Council of Canada, Fonds pour la Formation de Chercheurs et l'Aide à la Recherche, and the McConnell Fellowship Foundation of McGill University for their generous financial assistance. Sections two and three of MS McLennan 477 are published by kind permission of McGill University.

[2] Since the completion of this article my attention has been drawn by Dr Janet M. Hartley to two manuscripts in the Bodleian Library, Oxford, which are clearly related to MS McLennan 477. These are Selden supra 59, which contains what appears to be a duplicate of the translated *Sudebnik* forming the first section of MS McLennan 477, and Selden supra 60, which contains what may be a rough draft for this translation. The hand in Selden supra 60 is different from that in the McLennan 477 and Selden supra 59 translations, which is clearly that of a professional copyist. Selden supra 60 also includes an incomplete version of the third section of McLennan 477 (the outline of the Muscovite bureaucratic apparatus). Dr R. Cleminson has brought two further apparently related documents to my notice, namely Bodleian manuscripts Selden superius 112 (fols. 3–78) and Selden superius 113.

1

The manuscript is in the form of a small book measuring 10 cm. (width) by 15 cm. (length), with a spine 1 cm. wide on which are faintly visible the words 'The lawes of Russia written'. It is bound in vellum and sewn together with string. Two sets of thin leather ties are attached to the edges of the front and back covers—one at the bottom and one at the top. In all, the manuscript consists of forty-two leaves in gatherings of two leaves. Each side is ruled in identical fashion— two margins 1 cm. wide each on the left, one margin 1 cm. wide on the right, and one margin 1.5 cm. wide at the top and bottom. The margins are drawn in a ruddy-coloured ink, whereas that used in the actual text is black. The title, 'An Abridgement of the Russe Sowdebnik or Lawe booke', is on fol. 2^r. The text begins on fol. 3^r and continues (on both sides of each leaf) to fol. 41^r. Three blank, but ruled, sides (fols. 41^v, 42^r, 42^v) appear at the end. There are no catchwords.

Two distinct hands have been detected in the text. The first, in which almost all of the text is written, is a neat and somewhat ornate English secretary hand. The other, which appears in only a few instances in the second section of the manuscript, is hurried to the point of rendering certain words illegible and is totally lacking in elegance. Moreover, it always appears at the end of an entry, either providing a numerical figure or an additional English equivalent for a Russian term just explained. For instance, the entry 'Siny/Deti Bo-yarskie' (31^v) con- cludes with an addition in the second hand which reads, 'ther may be some 40000'; that on 'Torgovie choloveke' (34^v) ends with the addition of 'a market man' in the second hand. On three occasions an inscrut- able inscription precedes an entry in the second hand. It appears to read as 500^v following the entry 'Boyaren' (fol. 31^r), as 40^v following the entry 'Dvoranie' (fol. 31^v), and 20^v following the entry 'Siny/Deti Bo-yarskie' (fol. 31 v).

There is a watermark in the top left-hand corner of twenty-two of the manuscript's leaves, but in most cases it is almost completely lost in the binding or obscured by the text. It consists of an eagle with out- stretched wings and claws, a coat of arms down its centre, and a tail in a three-tiered curled motif from which is suspended a merchant mark consisting of the numeral 4 and the letters S and A. A watermark similar to this one is identified by Churchill as the 'Arms of Austria', dating from the seventeenth century. Briquet, however, includes several watermarks of similar design dating from the last few decades of the sixteenth century and appearing on paper of either German or Dutch provenance.[3]

[See p. 15 for n. 3]

Although the manuscript is neither signed nor dated and no firm conclusion as to its date can be based on the watermark, certain deductions can be made on the basis of internal evidence. In the second section, which lists and describes the various court, social, administrative, military, and clerical categories of Muscovite society, there appears a telling entry, namely 'Patriarkha' (patriarch) (fol. 35^r). Since the Russian patriarchate was established only in 1589, the manuscript must have been written after this date. Here we have our first clear-cut textual indicator of time.

From entries in the third section of the manuscript it is possible to reduce further the period during which the document must have been written. In this section, which lists and describes the various Muscovite chancelleries, forty-five officials are named, all but seven of whom have been identified. Of the thirty-eight officials who have been identified, eighteen are known from other sources to have served in the chancellery in which they appear in the manuscript. Among these crucial eighteen there are several prominent individuals about whose careers (including *dates* of appointment, removal, disgrace, etc.) we can speak with a fair degree of certainty.

The first of these individuals to provide us with a clue as to when the manuscript was written is Vasily Yakovlevich Shchelkalov. In the text, he appears as a *dumnyi d'yak* at the head of the *Posol'skii Prikaz* (Chancellery of Foreign Affairs), and in fact we know that he held both this rank and post. More importantly, however, we also know that he served as head of the *Posol'skii Prikaz* from 1594 (when he replaced his disgraced brother Andrey) to 1601, when he himself was disgraced and removed from office. The year 1601 also saw the purge of the Romanovs and their associates, among them the Prince Ivan Vasil'evich Sitsky, who was stripped of his boyar rank and banished to a remote monastery, where he died in 1608. He appears in the manuscript, however, as boyar in charge of the important *Prikaz Bol'shogo Prikhoda* (Chancellery of the Grand Revenue). Significant too is the fact that Ivan Vasil'evich Godunov, identified by the author as boyar at the head of the *Streletskii Prikaz* (Chancellery of Musketeers), died in 1601, and that Prince Mikhail Glebovich Saltykov, to whom the author ascribes the rank of *okol'nichii*, was promoted boyar in 1601. It would thus appear that the manuscript was written sometime after 1594, but certainly no later than 1601. Information on various other better-known individuals named by the author can assist us further.

Among these, there is a kinsman of Boris Godunov by the name of

³ W. A. Churchill, *Watermarks in Paper in Holland, England, France, etc. in the Seventeenth and Eighteenth Centuries and their Interconnection* (Amsterdam, 1965), p. ccxxxv (no. 282); C. M. Briquet, *Les Filigranes: Dictionnaire historique des marques du papier dès leur apparition vers 1282 jusqu'en 1600*, ed. A. Stevenson, 4 vols. (Amsterdam, 1968).

Stepan Vasil'evich Godunov. The author identifies him as *dvoretskii* or steward of the *Prikaz Bol'shogo Dvortsa* (Chancellery of the Grand Court). However, he was appointed *dvoretskii* only in 1598, following Boris Godunov's accession to the throne. Confirming 1598 as the earliest possible date of the manuscript's composition is the appointment that year of Afanasy Ivanov Vlas'ev as head of the *Prikaz Kazanskogo Dvortsa* (Kazan' Chancellery), in which capacity he appears in the manuscript. Our time-frame has thus contracted to 1598–1601.

In the year 1599, however, two events occurred, the results of which are not reported in the manuscript. First, the *d'yaki* Ivan Narmatsky and Postnik Dmitriev Lodygin were removed from the *Novyi Prikaz*, where they had served since this agency's creation in 1594, and replaced by one Mikhail Mikhailovich Saltykov. The author makes no mention of Saltykov in his description of the *Novyi Prikaz*, but does name Narmatsky and Lodygin as the *d'yaki* here. The second event of 1599 which assists our deductions is the death of the *dumnyi dvoryanin* Elezary Leont'evich Rzhevsky, whom the author names as head of the *Yamskoi Prikaz* (Post Chancellery). These two sets of information seem to suggest that the manuscript was written sometime in 1598 or 1599. Interestingly, however, Afanasy Ivanov Vlas'ev of the *Prikaz Kazanskogo Dvortsa* (see above) was appointed *dumnyi d'yak* (the rank which he holds in the manuscript) only in 1599. It would appear, then, that the manuscript was written *in 1599*, i.e. before the removal of Narmatsky and Lodygin from the *Novyi Prikaz* and before Rzhevsky's death, but after Vlas'ev's promotion to *dumnyi d'yak*.

2

The question of authorship, however, does not lend itself to a deductive procedure such as that used here to date the manuscript. Nevertheless, a certain amount of speculation is possible. The manuscript deals with matters significantly different from most other contemporary English works on Muscovy. It is not a traveller's account such as that of Richard Chancellor, Anthony Jenkinson, Jerome Horsey, or Giles Fletcher. This text, by contrast, consists of a translation of the Muscovite law code, and a terse and unadorned delineation of Muscovite society and government. Rather than a popular account intended for a wide audience, it appears to be an *aide-mémoire* directed to a small readership with an interest in Russia which went beyond the surface of things.

Who might this group have been? The work was perhaps commissioned by the Muscovy Company for reference by its members (primarily the agent) operating in Muscovy, for whom a clear and precise understanding of the legal norms of that society, as well as of the machinery of government, would have been useful. Or it may have originated from the intiative of some well-informed member, either for his own use or for that of his colleagues.[4] It is possible, too, that the English Government was somehow involved, although most certainly in conjunction with the Muscovy Company.[5]

Had the records of the Muscovy Company not perished in the Fire of London (1666) we might have been able to discover some reference there to the manuscript and to ascertain whether the author was a Company member or employee, and whether the document was ever circulated as a guide or *aide-mémoire*.[6] Having established, however, that the document was written in 1599, we can hazard some observations regarding Englishmen involved with Russia at that time who might have been in a position to produce such a work. Judging from the nature of the material included in the manuscript, we may say, to begin with, that its author seems to have had a fairly good knowledge of the Russian language, since the first section of his work is an English translation of the *Sudebnik*. Although this translation is far from perfect, it nevertheless displays a basic understanding of the general thrust of each article, as well as an impressive accuracy in the rendering of specific juridical terms and the description of prescribed legal procedure.[7] It is possible, however, that the author had some assistance at his disposal, either from a native Russian speaker or from a foreigner who was more conversant than he with Russian. It seems safe to assume, at the very least, that the author knew *some* Russian.

Another point worth bearing in mind is that the author must have had access to a copy of the *Sudebnik*. In view of the well-known Muscovite propensity to secrecy and suspicion of foreigners this was

[4] The Muscovy Company had been engaged in trade with Russia ever since its incorporation in 1555, following the so-called 'discovery of Russia' in 1553 by an English expedition seeking a north-east passage to the Indies. See T. S. Willan, *The Early History of the Russia Company 1553–1603* (Manchester, 1956), 1–18.

[5] My description of the manuscript's contents and the manner in which these are presented prompted Professor Samuel H. Baron to suggest that the work might represent an intelligence report prepared for the English Government or the Muscovy Company. Mr J. S. G. Simmons is also of the opinion that the manuscript appears to be diplomatic or connected with the Muscovy Company (private communications).

[6] The fact that the manuscript is in good physical condition—the cover and pages are not tattered, the pages are clean, the binding is intact—suggests that it was not widely circulated. It should be kept in mind, however, that the materials of which the manuscript is constructed are of superior quality and would not easily show wear.

[7] The extant copies of the *Sudebnik* differ from one another primarily in terms of textual variations deriving essentially from inattentiveness on the part of the copyists. The result is that the copies contain omissions, additions, misspellings, and misreadings which would, no doubt, have caused a translator some difficulty. For a discussion of these peculiarities, see B. D. Grekov (ed.), *Zekonodatel'nye pamyatniki russkogo tsentralizovannogo gosudarstva XV–XVII vekov: Sudebniki XV–XVI vekov* (M.–L., 1952), 113. The present evaluation of the author's translation is based on a comparison with the Russian version reproduced in this edition and with H. W. Dewey (ed.), *Muscovite Judicial Texts: 1488–1556*, Michigan Slavic Materials, No. 7 (Ann Arbor, 1966), *passim*.

probably not a simple matter. In all probability, such access would be more easily gained by someone who moved in high Muscovite circles, with contacts at court or among members of the élite at large, than by a simple merchant or mercenary.[8]

We may therefore direct our investigation towards Englishmen who are known to have had a knowledge of the Russian language and connections at court. The most obvious possibility would appear to be John Merrick, a seasoned observer of the Russian scene and an active participant in Anglo-Russian trade and diplomacy in the late sixteenth and early seventeenth centuries. The son of William Merrick (one of the original members of the Muscovy Company), John first arrived in Russia as an adolescent in 1573, when his father was appointed Company agent. He spent several years there learning his father's trade, as well as the Russian language, and in the periods 1592–1600 and 1605–12 he himself served as Company agent. Owing to his long experience in Muscovy and his fluency in the Russian language, Merrick was also involved to a considerable degree in diplomatic exchange between England and Russia, providing the English Government with invaluable information and insights into the state of affairs in Muscovy, as well as translating the tsar's letters and drafting appropriate English responses. In addition, he was on close and amicable terms with members of the court, including Boris Godunov (both before and after the latter's accession).[9]

Another candidate is Dr Mark Ridley, court physician to Tsar Fedor Ivanovich between 1594 and 1598, and author of the first English–Russian and Russian–English dictionaries. Several factors point to Ridley. To begin with, he was in Russia at just the right time. He began his stay in 1594 and, although his original commission at court ended with the death of Fedor Ivanovich in 1598, Elizabeth I's request to the new tsar Boris Godunov to allow Ridley to return to England indicates that Ridley left Russia only in April 1599.[10] Secondly, as the tsar's personal physician, he could well have had access to a copy of the *Sudebnik*. His constant presence in the heart of Moscow, moreover, near the tsar and among the bureaucrats and élite would have enabled him to garner information on the structure, responsibilities, and personnel of the Muscovite central administrative network of chancel-

[8] Earlier in the sixteenth century the diplomat Sigismund von Herberstein managed to examine the *Sudebnik* of 1497 and translated articles 3–7 and 9–16 (out of a total of 68) into Latin. See Sigismund von Herberstein, *Notes upon Russia*, trans. and ed. R. H. Major (London, 1851–2).

[9] '... he combined the commercial duties of a merchant and the political responsibilities of a diplomat so skillfully that he became the leader of the Muscovy Company and the chief architect of English governmental policy towards Russia.' See Geraldine Phipps, *Sir John Merrick: An English Merchant Diplomat in Seventeenth Century Russia* (Newtonville, 1983), p. i; see also T. S. Willan, *The Muscovy Merchants of 1555* (Manchester, 1953), 113–14.

[10] Gerald Stone, 'Mark Ridley (1560–1624): An Elizabethan Slavist', *Journal of Russian Studies*, liii (1987), 4.

leries, as well as on the general outlines of Muscovite society. Finally, as compiler of both an English–Russian and a Russian–English dictionary, he evidently had a mastery of the Russian language at least equal to that displayed in the manuscript.[11]

A comparison of hands might throw some light on the question of who wrote the manuscript: Merrick, Ridley, or perhaps someone else, but such a comparison would necessarily be inconclusive, as it is clear that the manuscript—except for a few scattered words—was written in the hand, not of the author, but of a professional copyist. The manuscript's second hand may be that of the author, but it appears far too seldom and is scrawled much too messily to serve as an adequate comparative sample.[12] However, Professor G. Phipps, Merrick's biographer,[13] tells me that the manuscript does not appear to be of the sort that Merrick, as she knows him, would have produced. She also informs me that Merrick left little in his own hand which might be used as the basis for a comparison.

As regards Dr Ridley, there is another approach that might assist us in determining whether he is connected in some way with the manuscript. This involves a comparison of the manuscript's English translation of Russian words, primarily from the *Sudebnik* section, with the translations of the same words in Ridley's dictionary. The results of this comparison are telling. For instance, Ridley mistranslates the word *yabednichestvo* 'false accusation' as 'burglarie'.[14] Interestingly, the same error is found in the manuscript. Of interest too are the terms *okol'nichii* and *dvoretskii*, which both Ridley and the manuscript have distorted in exactly the same fashion, namely as *okolnichen* and *dvoretsko*. It would seem that there are grounds for suggesting that Dr Mark Ridley was at least in some way linked with the manuscript.

There is also another interesting parallel. On fol. 42^r of Bodleian MS Laud misc. 47b (Ridley's English–Russian dictionary) the following words are faintly pencilled:

> Anni mundi Ruthenoru[m] 7058
> latinoru[m] 5511
> Christi 1549
> more then the latins by 1546

---

[11] Dr G. C. Stone of Hertford College, Oxford, is at present preparing for publication the three Bodleian manuscripts (Laud misc. 47a, Laud misc. 47b, and Selden supra 61) which constitute Ridley's dictionary. See Stone, 'Mark Ridley' (n. 10). The authorship of these manuscripts was first established by J. S. G. Simmons and B. O. Unbegaun in 'Slavonic Manuscript Vocabularies in the Bodleian Library', *Oxford Slavonic Papers*, ii (1951), 119–27.

[12] A comparison of hands including those in the Selden MSS (n. 2) might be more fruitful. This awaits the attention of a specialist.

[13] Cf. n. 9.

[14] I. I. Sreznevsky, *Materialy dlya slovarya drevne-russkogo yazyka*, 3 vols. (Spb., 1893–1903), s.v., gives no evidence to support this translation.

The significance of this becomes clear if we compare it with the manuscript's preamble to the translated *Sudebnik* (fol. 3ʳ):

The Lawes of Russia were made by Ivan Vasilivitch Emp. of Russia in the yeare from Adam as the greke church writeth *7058* but after [indecipherable word] of the latine church from the beginning of the Worlde *5511* which was in the year of Christ's incarnation *1549* . . . [emphasis mine, M.S.A.]

Taken alone, Ridley's note of the year 1549 is incomprehensible; there is no reason why Ridley should have been interested in this particular date. In conjunction with the manuscript, however, the inscription does assume a meaning. It appears to be a reference to the year in which the *Sudebnik* was completed, a reference which may reasonably be taken to link Ridley or his dictionary or both of them to the manuscript now under discussion.[15]

3

The second section of the manuscript deals with the Muscovite social and administrative hierarchy, presented under nine broad headings:

1. The degrees of Boyarskie or nobility in Russia next to the Tsare, Emp. or King, ghosodare or lorde Velike knez or gret Duke
2. Attenders for the Emps. privatt service
3. Principall Officers
4. Officers Millitarye
5. Officers abrode in Shires
6. The communalltye of Mowzhikes or unnoble in the cittie or goode towne
7. In the countrye villages
8. The Clargie
9. Monastaries Men

Subdivisions in transliterated Russian delineate what the author deemed the chief constituent parts, and it is in the subdivisions that the peculiarities of the Russian order are revealed.

Most of the entries into which each of the nine broad headings of this section are subdivided are accompanied by terse explanations. These explanations range from a one-word English equivalent to several lines. With a few exceptions, even these more substantial entries confine themselves to the minimum of information needed to differentiate one Muscovite group from another. Such brevity is consistent with the

[15] In both cases the year 7058 is equated with 1549, whereas 1549/1550 would have been a more precise equivalent. If, as is generally accepted, the *Sudebnik* was completed in June 7058, then 1550, not 1549, is the correct date of completion.

hypothesis that the manuscript was intended as a guide or manual, for it would have made sense, if this were the case, to keep the entries short and to the point, providing just enough information to facilitate the user's interaction with Russians from different walks of life, without confusing him with too many facts.

The entries on the boyar, *okol'nichii*, *dvoryanin*, and *syn boyarskii* are somewhat longer than the others, but the longest entry of all is that for the *gost'*. Since the *gosti* were the most important group among the Muscovite merchant community, this supports the suggestion that the manuscript was intended for the Muscovy Company or for some other commercial interests in Russia. Though brief, the entries have a broad coverage and are generally accurate. With few exceptions, all the major groups which constituted sixteenth-century Muscovite society are listed. The main exception are the *kholopy* 'slaves', who by the end of the sixteenth century formed a fairly numerous group in Muscovy.[16] It is therefore curious that there is no mention of them. The omission is all the more inexplicable in view of the fact that the *kholopy* are dealt with at considerable length in the *Sudebnik*[17] and are also referred to in the description of the functions of the *Kholopii Prikaz* (Slavery Chancellery).

Also missing are the *dumnye dvoryane* and *dumnye d'yaki*, but we may assume that the author knew of their existence since he describes certain individuals in the last section of the manuscript as 'dvoranin of the counsell' and 'secretarye of the counsell'. A further notable omission is the *konyushii* 'Master of the Horse'. Other observers of the Muscovite scene, including Antonio Possevino, Giles Fletcher, Jacques Margeret, and Grigory Kotoshikhin, not only mentioned this functionary, but also indicated that he was the most important of the courtiers, possessing great wealth and wielding considerable power.[18] This is the only major court office missing from the list. The omission must be an oversight, for we know that the office of *konyushii* during the period 1599–1601 was held by the boyar Dmitry Ivanovich Godunov.[19] The author's description of the remaining courtiers only mentions their ceremonial duties and ignores their political, diplomatic, and military responsibilities.

The third and final section of the manuscript centres on the

---

[16] Slaves were the second largest social group in Muscovy during the period 1450–1725, constituting about 10 per cent of the total population. See Richard Hellie, *Slavery in Russia, 1450–1725* (Chicago, 1982), 15.

[17] The *Sudebnik* of 1550 devotes thirteen articles to slavery-related issues, namely 35, 40, 63, 65–7, 76–81, 88.

[18] By the sixteenth century 'the post [of equerry] had become honorific and was the most powerful and lucrative position'. See Nancy Shields Kollman, *Kinship and Politics: The Making of the Muscovite Political System, 1345–1547* (Stanford, 1987), 95.

[19] N. Novikov (ed.), *Drevnyaya rossiiskaya vivliofika*, xx (Spb., 1791), 69–73.

Muscovite bureaucracy. Again, the treatment is concise and system-
atic, although the data are fuller than in the preceding section. The
heading 'The courtes and officers nowe in place in the Emps. castell att
Mosko' is followed by a list of twenty-four central administrative
departments, including both *prikazy* (chancelleries) and *chetverti* (tax-
collection agencies). Each department is identified by its Russian name
followed by a description of its responsibilities. The name of the official
heading each department is also given.

Earlier in the sixteenth century, Heinrich von Staden had compiled a
list of chancelleries,[20] but his descriptions are only cursory. It was, in
any case, not until the 1570s and 1580s that the Muscovite bureaucracy
really expanded, increasing the number of its chancelleries and extending its purview.[21] In his discussion of Russian administrative practices
during the reign of Fedor Ivanovich (1584–98), Giles Fletcher also
touches upon the chancelleries. In fact, he tells us a good deal about
them, but in such a confused fashion that his 'misconceptions have
compounded the difficulty of delineating the different chancelleries of
the late sixteenth century'.[22] Most of our sources on the Muscovite
bureaucracy, whether on the chancelleries or the officials who manned
them, date from the seventeenth century.[23]

The manuscript's information on the chancelleries is of two types.
The first concerns the responsibilities of a given chancellery; the second
deals with the chancellery's chief personnel. As mentioned above,
twenty-four chancelleries are named, but some of these receive only
cursory treatment. An extreme example is the *Chelobitnyi Prikaz*

[20] Staden's list of the 'foremost chancelleries' includes the following: (1) Service Land Chancellery, (2) Military Chancellery, (3) Treasury Chancellery, (4) Robbery Chancellery, (5) *Zemskii
Dvor*, (6) Post Chancellery, (7) Petitions Chancellery, (8) Chancellery of Kazan'/Astrakhan', (9)
Chancellery of Foreign Affairs. See Heinrich von Staden, *The Land and Government of Muscovy*,
trans. and ed. Thomas Esper (Stanford, 1967), 9–13.

[21] N. V. Ustyugov, 'Evolyutsiya prikaznogo stroya russkogo gosudarstva v XVII v.', in: *Abso-
lyutizm v Rossii (XV–XVIII vv.)*, ed. N. M. Druzhinin (M., 1964), 134; Peter Bowman Brown,
'Early Modern Russian Bureaucracy: The Evolution of the Chancellery System from Ivan III to
Peter the Great' (unpublished Ph.D. thesis, University of Chicago, 1978), 160. On the develop-
ment of the Muscovite bureaucracy in general, as well as on individual chancelleries, see also N. F.
Demidova, 'Byurokratizatsiya gosudarstvennogo apparata absolyutizma v XVII–XVIII vv.', in:
Druzhinin, *Absolyutizm*, pp. 206–42; A. K. Leont'ev, *Obrazovanie prikaznoi sistemy upravleniya v
russkom gosudarstve* (M., 1961); W. M. Pintner and D. K. Rowney (eds.), *Russian Officialdom: The
Bureaucratization of Russian Society from the Seventeenth to the Twentieth Century* (Chapel Hill, 1980);
I. I. Verner, *O vremeni i prichinakh obrazovaniya moskovskikh prikazov* (M., 1907–8); M. A. D'yakonov,
Ocherki obshchestvennogo i gosudarstvennogo stroya drevnei Rusi (Spb., 1908); S. B. Veselovsky,
'Prikaznoi stroi upravleniya moskovskogo gosudarstva', in: *Russkaya istoriya v ocherkakh i stat'yakh*,
ed. M. V. Dovnar Zapol'sky (Kiev, 1912), 164–98.

[22] Brown, op. cit. (n. 21), 203.

[23] The dearth of sixteenth-century sources on the Muscovite bureaucracy is attributable
primarily to a series of Moscow fires (1547, 1571, 1591, 1611, 1626). In general, we have more documents at our disposal for the Foreign Affairs, Service Land, Military, Siberian, and Robbery
chancelleries than for any others. For some chancelleries we have almost no documentation.
Leont'ev, *Obrazovanie* (n. 21), 17–19; Brown, op. cit. (n. 21), 130, 145–6.

(Petitions Chancellery), which is described simply as the 'office of requeste'. Fortunately, such examples are exceptional. Most of the entries outline the chancellery's main area of responsibility. For instance, under the entry for the *Posol'skii Prikaz* (Chancellery of Foreign Affairs), we are told that this chancellery handles not only Muscovy's relations with other states and matters of diplomatic protocol (e.g. the reception of foreign embassies, issuing of passes into and out of Muscovy, etc.), but also has under its jurisdiction the affairs of foreign merchants operating in Russia, and is the repository of the state seals.

The author being a visitor to Russia, it is perhaps not surprising that the entry on the *Posol'skii Prikaz* is so well-informed. Other entries, however, display the same kind of familiarity. The entry on the *Pomestnyi Prikaz* (Service Land Chancellery) is especially interesting. Here, in addition to outlining the responsibilities of this chancellery, the author describes both the service requirements and compensation rates for Muscovite military men. In his account of the *Streletskii Prikaz* (Chancellery of Musketeers), he tells us how much the musketeers are paid, and the form of payment (grain and cloth as well as money). The entry on the *Kazennyi Dvor* (Treasury Chancellery) provides details of the luxuries stored in the Treasury, as well as of the manner in which Treasury officials procure these goods. The entry on the *Yamskoi Prikaz* (Post Chancellery) describes its handling of dispatches as well as the men who run the postal stations and their remuneration. Such information may add little that is new to our knowledge of Muscovite bureaucracy and society, but it confirms many of our hypotheses, which, owing to the dearth of Muscovite material, were hitherto often based on scanty or inconclusive evidence. Moreover, it helps to give us a clearer picture of what exactly the English knew about Russia.

There are three matters, however, on which the manuscript sheds significant new light. The first is the number of chancelleries in existence at the end of the sixteenth century. Other sources available to us indicate the existence of twenty-three chancelleries by the time of Ivan IV's death in 1584, and an estimated thirty-one by the end of the century.[24] Of these thirty-one chancelleries, all but ten appear in the manuscript's list.[25] The missing ten may have escaped the author's

[24] The source for these figures is the Appendix to Brown, op. cit. (n. 21), which provides a list of all known chancelleries from the second half of the fifteenth to the first half of the eighteenth century.

[25] The missing ten chancelleries are: (1) *Aptekarskii Prikaz* (Apothecary Chancellery), (2) *Bronnyi Prikaz* (Weapons Production Chancellery), (3) *Koniushennyi Prikaz* (Equerry Chancellery), (4) *Novgorodskii Dvortsovyi Prikaz* (Novgorod Court Chancellery), (5) *Pechatnyi Dvor* (Book-Printing Chancellery), (6) *Postel'nyi Prikaz* (Bedchamber Chancellery), (7) *Oruzheinaya Palata* (Armoury Chancellery), (8) *Sudnyi Moskovskii Prikaz* (Moscow Judicial Chancellery), (9) *Sudnyi Vladimirskii Prikaz* (Vladimir Judicial Chancellery), (10) *Kabatskii Prikaz* (Excise Tax Chancellery).

notice, or were perhaps irrelevant to his purposes. Another possibility is that the author considered them to be sub-branches of chancelleries which he does mention. More significant than the absence of these missing chancelleries, however, is the inclusion of three others which are generally thought to have been established during the seventeenth, not the sixteenth, century. These are: the *Chetvert'* (Tax-Collection Agency) for Siberia, the *Panskii Prikaz* (Chancellery of Foreign Mercenaries), and the *Tamozhennyi Prikaz* (Customs Tax Chancellery).

The second matter on which the manuscript appears to throw new light is the social status of the personnel heading the chancelleries. Several historians have argued that, during the sixteenth century, the chancelleries were headed predominantly by the state secretaries, i.e. *d'yaki* and, in some cases, *dumnye d'yaki*.[26] Boyars, *okol'nichie*, and *dumnye dvoryane*, they say, served primarily in the military establishment, and when they did become involved in civil affairs, it was in the area of provincial administration and not the chancelleries. It is asserted that this was a time when warriors and bureaucrats rarely, if ever, strayed into each other's territory.[27] On the few occasions when *duma* members other than the *dumnye d'yaki* did head chancelleries during the sixteenth century, it is held that these were, as a rule, only 'second-level *prikazy*'.[28] This situation changed, however, during the seventeenth century, when more and more *duma* members were appointed heads of chancelleries, thus effecting the emergence of what Crummey has termed the 'noble official'.[29]

Though this is now the prevalent view, Klyuchevsky was of the opinion that *duma* members other than the *dumnye d'yaki* in fact administered the most important of the chancelleries (except for the *Razryadnyi, Pomestnyi*, and *Posol'skii Prikazy*) throughout the sixteenth century.[30] More recently, Skrynnikov has endorsed the view that a number of sixteenth-century chancelleries were under the supervision of non-bureaucrats, i.e. prominent courtiers or *duma* members.[31] Crummey's response to Skrynnikov's assertion is that, if certain chancelleries were indeed in the hands of non-bureaucrats, these must have been only a few in number and, for the most part, only fledgeling chancelleries, i.e. court departments in the process of evolving into *prikazy*.[32]

[26] Robert O. Crummey, 'The Origins of the Noble Officials: The Boyar Elite, 1613–1689', in: Pintner and Rowney, *Russian Officialdom* (n. 21), 47; Demidova, 'Byurokratizatsiya' (n. 21), 208–9; Borivoj Plavsic, 'Seventeenth Century Chanceries and Their Staffs', in: Pintner and Rowney, *Russian Officialdom* (n. 21), 39; Brown, op. cit. (n. 21), 76.

[27] Crummey, loc. cit. (n. 26).

[28] Demidova, 'Byurokratizatsiya' (n. 21), 208–9.

[29] Robert O. Crummey, *Aristocrats and Servitors: The Boyar Elite in Russia, 1613–1689* (Princeton, 1983), 34–64.

[30] V. O. Klyuchevsky, *Kurs russkoi istorii*, ii (M.-L., 1923), 421, 428.

[31] R. G. Skrynnikov, *Ivan Groznyi* (M., 1975), 192.

[32] Crummey, 'Origins' (n. 26), 47.

The manuscript, however, paints quite a different picture. A close look at the chancellery personnel named by the author indicates that, in 1599–1601, a large number of chancelleries were in fact headed by non-bureaucrats. Of the twenty-four chancelleries named, twelve were administered by either boyars, *okol'nichie*, or *dumnye dvoryane* (eight boyars, two *okol'nichie*, and two *dumnye dvoryane*). Moreover, these non-bureaucrats were directing the affairs not of second-level or fledgeling chancelleries, but of important departments, such as the *Bol'shoi Prikhod* or *Streletskii Prikaz*.

As indicated above, there are ten chancelleries missing from the manuscript's list. If we assume that each of these chancelleries was headed by a *d'yak*, that would mean that 35 per cent of all chancelleries known to us in the closing years of the sixteenth century were run by non-bureaucrats. However, it is possible that some of the missing chancelleries too were actually under the supervision of non-bureaucrats. It seems likely, for instance, that the *Postel'nyi Prikaz* (Bedchamber Chancellery), *Konyushennyi Prikaz* (Equerry Chancellery), and *Aptekarskii Prikaz* (Apothecary Chancellery), since they concerned the tsar personally, were run by courtiers, perhaps *duma* members. This would bring the proportion of chancelleries headed by non-bureaucrats up to at least 44 per cent. It appears from this that the involvement of courtiers and *duma* members in chancellery affairs began at least as early as the end of the sixteenth century, as Klyuchevsky and Skrynnikov maintain.

The late A. A. Zimin devoted a good deal of attention to the Muscovite élite, in an attempt to acquire a clearer picture of the functioning of the Muscovite political system. He believed that it was virtually impossible to make any real sense of this system, in particular of the role of the *duma*, without first establishing the composition of the élite.[33] Gustave Alef took Zimin's proposition one step further, observing that 'A better way of assessing the role played by the *duma*, given the relative absence of contemporary commentaries, would be to discover the *functions* assigned to its members' (emphasis mine, M.S.A.).[34]

The manuscript points precisely to such functions, i.e. élite appointments to chancellery headships. It suggests that the *duma* was more than just a gathering of prominent servitors of great wealth and illustrious family. Owing to the presence of the heads of the most important of the central administrative departments it was something more akin to what Klyuchevsky described, namely a 'council of ministers'.[35] The extent to which the tsar heeded the counsel of his 'ministers' obviously

[33] A. A. Zimin, 'Sostav boyarskoi dumy v XV–XVI vekakh', in: *Arkheograficheskii ezhegodnik za 1957 god*, ed. M. N. Tikhomirov (M., 1958), 41.
[34] Gustave Alef, 'Reflections on the Boyar Duma in the Reign of Ivan III', *Slavonic and East European Review*, xlv (1967), 80.
[35] Klyuchevsky, *Kurs* (n. 30), 428–9.

cannot be ascertained on the basis of the information provided by the manuscript; but it does testify to a potentially important—even central—role for the *duma* in governing the Muscovite state in the late sixteenth century.

The third question on which the manuscript proves useful is that of the activities of the individuals named therein. As was mentioned above, most of our data on the chancelleries, including that on their personnel (*prikaznye lyudi*), date from the seventeenth century. Here, we have an earlier source which displays a truly impressive familiarity with the bureaucratic personnel of the late sixteenth century. Of the forty-five chancellery officials named, eighteen (40 per cent) can be traced in other sources to the chancellery in which they appear in the manuscript. Significantly, of the twenty-seven officials who cannot be traced in this way, not one can be located elsewhere in the period 1599–1601. The sources I have consulted either contain no information at all on these individuals in the period 1599–1601 or comment exclusively on court or military assignments, not chancellery service. The information on these twenty-seven officials provided by the manuscript thus appears to fill in a gap in the existing data.

APPENDIX 1

Section Two of 'The Lawes of Russia Written'

The degrees of Boyarskie or nobility in Russia next to the Tsare, Emp. or King, ghosodare [*gosudar'*] or lorde Velike knez [*velikii knyaz'*] or gret Duke[36]

31ʳ Boyaren [*boyarin*], a counseller magistrate or best nobleman of the best bloode and landes, ther be aboute Twentye of them all of the counsell,[37] and one is made Bolshoi or cheife that hath onelye accesse to the Emp. and giveth the ffinal Sentence in counsell.[38] 500ᵛ[?] They ar about 20 in all

Okolnichen [*okol'nichii*], is a degree lower and some be of the counsell which attend neere the prince and counsell to goe aboute such matters as be committed to them,[39] an harbenger, they ar about a dozen ||

---

[36] The spelling, capitalization, and punctuation of the original are retained throughout. To assist the reader, however, standardized transliterations of Russian terms are added in square brackets.

[37] For the testimony of other witnesses on the boyars, see Edward A. Bond (ed.), *Russia at the Close of the Sixteenth Century* (London, 1856), 29, 36; Hugh F. Graham (ed.), *The Moscovia of Antonio Possevino* (Pittsburgh, 1977), 11; and Novikov, op. cit. (n. 19), 70–1.

[38] This is probably a reference to the *pervosovetnik*. See G. Vernadsky, *Political and Diplomatic History of Russia* (Boston, 1936), 188.

[39] This may be a reference to the fact that some *okol'nichie* were on hand to attend *duma* sessions, while others were away on assignment. It is also possible, however, that a distinction is being drawn between those *okol'nichie* consulted by the tsar at *duma* sessions only and those closer to the tsar, with whom he would also meet privately and informally outside the *duma*, i.e. the *blizhnie*. On the latter, see G. O. Kotoshikhin, *O Rossii v tsarstvovanie Alekseya Mikhailovicha* (Spb., 1906), 25.

Dvoranie [*dvoryanin*], a courtier, they be pensioners or squires to attend to be 31[v] imployed as governors and iustices in Shires, keepers of casteles, messengers to fforraine princes and captaines in the feild.[40] 40[v][?] ther may be about 200[41]

Siny/Deti Bo-yarskie [*syny/deti boyarskie*] boiars, gentellmen which are imployed as sergents & officialls to governers in Shires and castles and for light horsemen in the feild. 20[v][?] ther may be some 40000[42]

Knez [*knyaz'*], is an hereditarie tearme of honor prefixed before the name of some ancient gentellman, and according to ther lands and favour with the Emp, they be ranged in the former degrees. The woman is knina [*knyaginya*]. Vich is a termination of honor added to the end of the fathers name, soe is Vna for the woman, as Borris fedorovich: Maria Gregoriovna[43] ||

Attenders for the Emps. privatt service 32[r]

Stolnikes [*stol'nik*], ar Boyarens sonnes which attend one the Emp. Table and carrye meate from the dore to the Table.[44] 20[?] in all[45]

Strapchas [*stryapchii*], be the best squires sonnes that bring the dishes from the cookes to the princes dynynge chamber dore[46]

Sitniks [*sytnik*], fetch drinks from the buttery to the strapchas

Postelnike [*postel'nichii* or *postel'nik*], he keepeth the Emp. bedd and governeth the zhiltsi and is of the counsel and a dvoranine[47]

Zhiletse or zhiltsie [*zhilets*] be dvoronins sonnes that are lodged neere the chamberlayne to be sent of arrante ||

Stopnikes [*istopnik*] they fetch such thinges as be necessarye for the Emps. use and 32[v] over seeth the storowzhes to heat the stoves and to keepe the galleryes cleine from snowe

[40] The *dvoryane* were first and foremost warriors, constituting the bulk of Muscovy's armed forces until the second half of the seventeenth century. See R. Hellie, *Enserfment and Military Change in Muscovy* (Chicago, 1971); A. A. Zimin, *Reformy Ivana Groznogo* (M., 1960); and Kotoshikhin, *O Rossii* (n. 39), 41–2.

[41] Hellie (*Enserfment* (n. 40), 267) estimates that, at the end of the sixteenth century, the *dvoryane* and *deti boyarskie* taken together numbered some 25,000.

[42] Cf. n. 41.

[43] Boris Fedorovich and Mariya Grigor'evna were the names and patronymics of Boris Godunov and his wife. For other travellers' notes on patronymics, see Bond, *Russie* (n. 37), 38; and Lloyd E. Berry and Robert Crummey (eds.), *Rude and Barbarous Kingdom: Russia in the Accounts of Sixteenth-Century Voyagers* (Madison, 1968), 93. Boris Fedorovich is also the example used by Giles Fletcher (Bond, loc. cit.).

[44] Court service was not the primary function of the *stol'niki*. They were engaged in a whole series of military, civil, and diplomatic activities, either as assistants to higher-ranking officials or as heads of chancelleries and military units. They also constituted part of the tsar's regiment during military campaigns. See Kotoshikhin, *O Rossii* (n. 39), 25; Hellie, *Enserfment* (n. 40), 23; and I. Zabelin, *Domashnii byt russkogo naroda* (M., 1895), *passim*.

[45] The manuscript is difficult to read at this point. If the figure is indeed 20, it is surprising, for Kotoshikhin (*O Rossii* (n. 39), 25) says there were about 500 *stol'niki* in the second half of the seventeenth century.

[46] On the *stryapchie*, see Kotoshikhin, *O Rossii* (n. 39), 25; Zabelin, *Domashnii byt* (n. 44), *passim*; and Hellie, *Enserfment* (n. 40), 23.

[47] During the late 1590s, the post of *postel'nichii* was held by one Istoma Osipovich Bezobrazov, who had served in the same capacity under both Ivan IV and Fedor Ivanovich, but whether he was a *dumnyi dvoryanin* at this time, as the author indicates, is not known. See Kotoshikhin, *O Rossii* (n. 39), 29; and Novikov, op. cit. (n. 19), 69–69.

Storowzhe [*storozh*] he is a poore watchman to heat the ovens and to performe all the meane offices.

Principall Officers

Dvoretsko [*dvoretskii*], the steward of the princes crowne lands and howse, and is the Emps. Taster

Kaznachee [*kaznachei*], Treasuer [*sic*]

Pechatnike [*pechatnik*], the keeper of the gret and small seale ||

33ʳ   Diake [*d'yak*], a clarke that hath a Boyaren or a secretarie of the counsell or embasador above him in commyssion

Podiach [*pod'yachii*], an under clarke that is ioyned either with a dvoranine or a diake

Pristave [*pristav*], he that giveth attendance on embassendors or messengers or hath the custodie of anye

Nadelchike [*nedel'shchik*], a sergent

Yezdoke [*ezdok*], a Bayley arrant[48]

Officers Millitarye

Voyavode [*voevoda*], a generall or conquerer[49]

Gholova [*golova*], a gret captayne that hath other captaines under him, a coronell ||

33ᵛ   Sotnike [*sotnik*], a captaine of an hundered, a constable

Patdesatnike [*pyatidesyatnik*], a captaine of ffiftye, a corporall, a sergeant

Officers abrode in Shires

Namestnike [*namestnik*], a liuetenant, a governour

Volostele [*volostel'*], a Towne rive

Tiyune [*tiun*], a deputie assistant to the cheif officer

Tamoshnike [*tamozhennyi tseloval'nik*], a customer who is a citizen of Mosko[50]

Starost [*starosta*] a Bayley[51]

Chelovanike [*tseloval'nik*] a sworne man[52] ||

---

[48] The powers of the *ezdok* were not generally as wide as those of the 'bayley arrant', who performed the same types of duties as the sergeant, or, in the Russian context, the *nedel'shchik*. See Brown, op. cit. (n. 21), 129; and *OED*, s.v.

[49] On the *voevoda*, see Bond, *Russia* (n. 37), 73; and J. Margeret, *Capitaine Jacques Margeret, un mousquetaire à Moscou: Mémoires sur la première révolution russe, 1604–1614*, ed. A. Bennigsen (Paris, 1983), 75.

[50] By the end of the sixteenth century the *gosti* had moved into the spheres of state finances, serving among other capacities, as customs officers. They were, as a rule, required to take up residence in Moscow. This may explain the words 'cittizen of Mosko'. See Samuel H. Baron, 'Who Were the Gosti?', *California Slavic Studies*, vii (1973), 7.

[51] The form of this word used by Giles Fletcher to translate *starosta* is 'bailief' (Bond, *Russia* (n. 37), 29, 36).

[52] The *tseloval'nik* was an official elected by the rural and urban communities of Muscovy to assist the *starosta* (also elected) in the management of local affairs, the administration of justice, and the collection of taxes, customs, and dues of various kinds. See Hellie, *Enserfment* (n. 40), 71; and R. E. F. Smith, *The Enserfment of the Russian Peasantry* (Cambridge, 1968), 104–5.

The communalltye of Mowzhikes [*muzhiki*] or unnoble in the cittie or goode   34ʳ
town

Cowpetse [*kupets*], a buyer, the best kinde of marchant

Ghost [*gost'*], a marchant to farr places ther be 12 in Mosko called the Emps. marchante,[53] who after they are growen to wealth offer a large present to the Emp.[54] and he taketh them to be his marchante and giveth them againe a gowne of cloth of golde and Timber of sables[55] to lyne it, this gowne they are called to weare at court when embassendors are heard, or one some gret festivall daye[56] ||

Torgovie choloveke [*torgovoi chelovek*], a lesse marchant, a cheapman, a market man   34ᵛ

Lavoshnike [*lavochnik*], a Shope keeper

Maister [*master*], an artificer

In the countrye villages

Christiyanine [*krest'yanin*], is a countrye man that is bound to the grounde to till it he and his posteritie who tilleth the cheife quantatye for the prince or nobleman, and hath a portion for the mayntynance of his familye and cattell[57]

Selskoi [*sel'skoi*] a ffarmer ||

Pashenike [*pashnik*] a plowe man   35ʳ

Pastowkhe [*pastukh*] a feeder or keeper of cattell

The Clargie

Patriarkha [*patriarkh*], the patriake of Mosko

Metrapolita [*mitropolit*], a metrapolitan, ther be towe[58]

Archiyepiskop [*arkhiepiskop*], an archbishope, fower[59]

---

[53] In 1598 there seem to have been at least twenty-one *gosti* in Muscovy, judging from the number of *gosti* signatures which appear on the resolution of the *Zemskii Sobor* convened in that year to decide upon the election of a new tsar following the death of Fedor Ivanovich. See P. Bushkovitch, *The Merchants of Moscow, 1580–1650* (New York, 1980), 17.

[54] This confirms the importance of wealth in rising to the rank of *gost'*.

[55] A 'timber' is a set of forty skins. See T. Wright, *Dictionary of Obsolete and Provincial English*, ii (1893), 963; and *OED*, s.v.

[56] The tsar used to lend finery from the Treasury to the *gosti* (as well as to courtiers) so that they might appear in splendid apparel during court ceremonies, especially when he was receiving foreign embassies. The Englishman Henry Lane, presented to the tsar at court in 1555 along with Richard Chancellor and Richard Killingsworth, reported that he saw in the Kremlin 'grave personages decked out in gorgeous apparel', some of whom turned out to be 'merchants of credit'. S. Baron, 'Ivan the Terrible, Giles Fletcher, and the Muscovite Merchantry', *Slavonic and East European Review*, lvi (1978), 568. See also Margeret, op. cit. (n. 49), 74.

[57] This confirms that by the end of the sixteenth century serfdom had come to Muscovy, in practice if not in law. Cf. Hellie, *Enserfment* (n. 40), 96–105; R. E. F. Smith, *Peasant Farming in Muscovy* (Cambridge, 1977), 108–9; G. T. Robinson, *Rural Russia Under the Old Regime* (Los Angeles, 1967), 13; and J. Blum, *Lord and Peasant in Russia from the Ninth to the Nineteenth Century* (New York, 1968), 254–62.

[58] When the Metropolitan of Moscow was elevated to the patriarchal throne in 1589, four archbishops were simultaneously consecrated metropolitans. These were the archbishops of Kazan', Rostov, Novgorod, and Krutitsy (a Moscow suburb). However, both Fletcher and the author state that there were only two metropolitans. This is either an error on their part or an indication that only two sees were occupied at the time. See Berry and Crummey, op. cit. (n. 43), 211; and Bond, *Russia* (n. 37), 108.

[59] The creation of the Patriarchate and elevation of four archbishops to the level of metropolitan

Yepiskop or vladike [*episkop/vladyka*], a bishobe, 6[60]
Protopope [*protopop*], the cheife preist who is the Emp. confessor[61]
Pope [*pop*], a preist
Diakon [*d'yakon*], a decon; These men be maried men.
Podiache, querristers[62] ||

35ᵛ   Monasteries Men

Archmandrita [*arkhimandrit*], an abbot
Ighowmen [*igumen*], a prior
Chernech [*chernets*], a fryer
Sveshenike [*svyashchennik*], the fryers prest
Chernitsa [*chernitsa*], a nunne

APPENDIX 2

Section Three of 'The Lawes of Russia Written'

The courtes and officers nowe in place in the Emps. castell att Mosko

Bolshoi Dvoretse [*Prikaz Bol'shogo Dvortsa*], or office of the receiving of the rente of the princes land, payeth the familye ther wages,[63] hath for the Boyaren over it the dvoretsko or Steward on Stepan Vasilevich Godonove,[64] the diak under him is Smirnoi Vasoliyeve[65] thes iudg all contraversies betweene Monastaries and friers.[66] The steward is all waies the Emp. Taster and is cheife over the stolnikes

in 1589 was accompanied by the establishment of the archbishoprics of Nizhnii Novgorod, Ryazan', Tver', Smolensk, Suzdal', and Vologda. Fletcher (Bond, *Russia* (n. 37), 108) says there were six archbishops. See also Berry and Crummey, op. cit. (n. 43), 211.

[60] After 1589 Muscovy had eight bishoprics: Kolomna, Pskov, Rzhev, Ustyug Velikii, Beloozero, Bryansk, Dmitrov, and an unnamed see. Both Fletcher (Bond, *Russia* (n. 37), 108) and the manuscript give the number of bishops as six. See also Berry and Crummey, op. cit. (n. 43), 108.

[61] Of the many archpriests, one was appointed by the tsar to be his confessor. See Berry and Crummey, op. cit. (n. 43), 140.

[62] The author must be referring here to the *d'yachok*, who, in addition to reading and singing during divine service, often served as rural clerk (*pod'yachii*). See S. Pushkarev, *Dictionary of Russian Historical Terms from the Eleventh Century to 1917* (New Haven, 1970), 12.

[63] This presumably refers to the royal family.

[64] On Stepan Vasil'evich Godunov, who was appointed *dvoretskii* in 1598 by his kinsman, tsar Boris Godunov, see Zimin, 'Sostav' (n. 33), 78; R. G. Skrynnikov, *Rossiya posle oprichniny* (L., 1975), 104–5; Berry and Crummey, op. cit. (n. 43), 155; S. F. Platonov, *Ocherki po istorii smuty v moskovskom gosudarstve, XVI–XVII vv.* (Spb., 1901), 207; and Isaac Massa, *A Short History of the Beginnings of these Present Wars in Moscow under the Reign of Various Sovereigns down to the Year 1610*, ed. G. Edward Orchard (Toronto, 1982), 108.

[65] Smirnoy Vasil'ev was a *d'yak* at the *Bol'shoi Dvorets* between 1596 and 1610. He was removed from this post in 1610 by order of King Sigismund of Poland, and replaced by one Mikhail T'yukhin. See S. B. Veselovsky, *D'yaki i pod'yachie XV–XVII vekov* (M., 1975), 85.

[66] The *Bol'shoi Dvorets* was involved in monastery affairs at least as early as 1551, when the *Stoglav* council decreed that '. . . a monastery's treasury and all material resources of monasteries will be under the authority of the tsar's and grand prince's major-domos [*dvoretskie*], who will be sent to audit, to take inventory, and to make remittances according to the books . . . of each

Posolskoy Prikaze [*Posol'skii Prikaz*], or office of embassages hath Vasilie Yakovlevich Schelkalove[67] for cheif diake or secretarye of counsell and state.[68] The diak or clarke under him is Ivan Ondree,[69] this man manageth all matters with fforraine || princes, and giveth embassators ther intertaynement and dispatch and doth the gretest biussines at home, keepeth the seales, and governeth on of the five provences of the lande,[70] alsoe he iudgeth over all fforraine marchant receiveth knowledge of all ther comodities dicideth ther actons and giveth letters to an froo and ther passes out of the land

Raizrade [*Razryad/Razryadnyi prikaz*], marshall or constable is Sapowne Abramove[71] a diake or secretarye of counsell and estate, and his diake is Istoma Kartashove,[72] he manageth all the nobilitie & gentrie of the lande who are employed all of them everye yeare either in service in the feild or in goverment at home, and are changed contynuallye the second or third yeare from on place to another[73] he hath alsoe a province of the land[74] ||

Pomestnoi prikaze [*Pomestnyi Prikaz*], hath for his diak Yelezarie Veilowzgyne[75] his

monastery'. See Donald Ostrowski, 'Church Polemics and Monastic Land Acquisition in Sixteenth Century Muscovy', *Slavonic and East European Review*, lxiv (1986), 371.

[67] Vasily Yakovlevich Shchelkalov was appointed director of the *Posol'skii Prikaz* in 1594, replacing his brother Andrey who had fallen into disfavour with the powerful Boris Godunov. He remained at this post until 1601, when he too fell into disgrace. See Veselovsky, *D'yaki* (n. 65), 588; Massa, *Short History* (n. 64), 36; *Russkii biograficheskii slovar'*, xxiv (1912), 46; Zimin, 'Sostav' (n. 33), 80; S. A. Belokurov, *O posol'skom prikaze* (M., 1906), 30–2; A. A. Zimin, *Oprichnina Ivana Groznogo* (M., 1964), 179, 295, 377; N. P. Likhachev, *Razryadnye d'yaki XVI veka* (Spb., 1888), 554–6; and Brown, op. cit. (n. 21), 191–2, 204, 207.

[68] 'secretarye of counsell and state' must mean *dumnyi d'yak*. Shchelkalov was appointed *dumnyi d'yak* in 1572. See Zimin, 'Sostav' (n. 33), 80.

[69] This individual has not been identified.

[70] This is the first of five references made by the author to a province of the land being under the supervision of the head of a chancellery. What exactly the author means by 'governeth' is not clear, but he seems to be echoing Fletcher's claim that the Muscovite state was divided into parts (Fletcher calls them 'chetfirds') which were assigned for supervision to individual chancelleries, i.e. the *Posol'skii Prikaz*, *Razryadnyi Prikaz*, *Pomestnyi Prikaz*, and *Prikaz Kazanskogo Dvortsa*. The author adds the *Sibirskaya Chetvert'* to this list. According to Fletcher, the heads of the chancelleries assigned to the 'chetfirds' were not involved in the actual day-to-day running of these territorial units, but merely received reports concerning their administration and the collection of dues and taxes from lesser officials appointed from Moscow, which they passed on to the tsar at *duma* sessions. This may be what is meant by the word 'governeth'. See G. Fletcher, *Of the Russe Commonwealth*, ed. R. Pipes and J. F. Fine Jr. (Cambridge, Mass., 1966), 29–37.

[71] This is Vasily (Sapunets) Tikhonovich Abramov (or Avramov), who was posted to the *Razryadnyi Prikaz* in 1583/4 and served there until the false Dmitry's accession to the throne in 1605. He was appointed *dumnyi d'yak* in 1593/4. The last mention of Abramov is in 1609, when he was serving as *voevoda* in Karelia. See *Russkii biograficheskii slovar'*, i (1896), 46–7; Likhachev, *Razryadnye d'yaki* (n. 67), 495–6; Veselovsky, *D'yaki* (n. 65), 9; and Berry and Crummey, op. cit. (n. 43), 147.

[72] Istoma Zakhar'evich Kartashev served as *pod'yachii* at the *Razryadnyi Prikaz* between 1587/8 and 1592/3. In 1596/7 he appears in this same *prikaz* but in the capacity of *d'yak*, and remains here until the coronation of the false Dmitry in 1605. Dmitry's usurper Vasily Shuisky reinstated Kartashev to his former position, which he then held until 1610. See Veselovsky, *D'yaki* (n. 65), 230.

[73] Staden too observed that *voevody* were transferred from place to place every two years or so. See Staden, op. cit. (n. 20), 8.

[74] Cf. n. 70.

[75] Elezary Vyluzgin was *dumnyi d'yak* in the *Pomestnyi Prikaz* between 1587 and 1601. During this period, he also participated in several foreign embassies, served on the committee investigating the

diak is Ivan Yefanove,[76] this secretarie of counsell and estate taketh notice of all the princes free holdes[77] which are bestowed upon his nobilitie and gentrie for the mayntynance of ther diett att home and in the warres. The Boyaren is rated to have a Thousand acres, the Dvoranine six hundred acres and the sin boyarskie three hundered[78] for which they are charged personallye to searve in the feild or else where in the government with tow horsemen or on at the least for an hunddred acres,[79] against the Crime Tarter ther contynualle enimye or against any other, alsoe inheritances[80] and monastaries lands[81] are charged to send to the feild according to this rate, he desideth all the contraversies of ther farmes & ther trespasses, he hath a provence of the land under him[82] ||

Kazanskoi Dvore [*Prikaz Kazanskogo Dvortsa*], hath Ofanasey Ivanove Vlasove[83] for diake who is a secretarie of counsell and estate and hath all the biusnes of the kingdome of Cazan and Astracan under him[84]

Nova Chetvert [*Novyi Prikaz/Novgorodskaya Chet'*] or newe province hath tow diakes

---

death of Tsarevich Dmitry of Uglich, and was involved in handling the purge of the Romanovs and their associates at court. See Likhachev, *Razryadnye d'yaki* (n. 67), 181, 184; V. I. Buganov (ed.), *Razryadnye knigi 1475–1598* (M., 1966), 443, 522; and idem (ed.), *Razryadnye knigi 1559–1605* (M., 1974), 330.

[76] Ivan Efanov served as *d'yak* at the *Pomestnyi Prikaz* in the period 1595–1605, and again in 1609–11. He was in this *prikaz* in the capacity of *pod'yachii* in 1584–6 and 1592–5. See Veselovsky, *D'yaki* (n. 65), 177–8.

[77] i.e. *pomest'ya*.

[78] The compensation scale for military servitors provided by the author closely accords with that known from other sources to have been in use towards the end of the sixteenth century, if we take the author's 'acres' to signify *chetverti*. For details, see Hellie, *Enserfment* (n. 40), 36, 290.

[79] According to the *Ulozhenie o sluzhbe* of 1556 each military servitor was required to provide one fully armed horseman (two for a distant campaign) for every 100 *chetverti* of land (per field in a three-field system, i.e. for every 300 *chetverti*). See ibid. 38.

[80] i.e. *votchiny*.

[81] It is interesting that the author subjects monasteries to the service requirements of the military establishment, for as far as is known from other sources, monasteries were exempt from these requirements (which may account for the State's preoccupation, during the sixteenth century, with preventing the Church from accumulating more land). It is true, however (and perhaps this is what the author is referring to), that monasteries were expected (and at times compelled) to share their vast resources with the State, especially during wartime. These contributions came in the form of cash, goods, and troops. See Ostrowski, 'Church Polemics' (n. 66), 376; and Hellie, *Enserfment* (n. 40), 43.

[82] Cf. n. 70.

[83] Afanasy Ivanov Vlas'ev (appointed *dumnyi d'yak* in 1599) was head of the *Prikaz Kazanskogo Dvortsa* in 1598–1603. He was also, as head of the *Posol'skii Prikaz* in 1601–6, prominent in diplomatic affairs. After the death of Boris Godunov, he found favour with the false Dmitry, who appointed him 'keeper of all the Tsar's treasure' and sent him to Poland to fetch his bride Maryna Mniszek. Upon becoming tsar, Vasily Shuisky removed Vlas'ev from his posts and had him sent to Ufa. In 1611, however, he was recalled to Moscow by Sigismund of Poland, elevated to the rank of *dumnyi dovryanin*, and reappointed *kaznachei*. See Likhachev, *Razryadnye d'yaki* (n. 67), 415; Vesselovsky, *D'yaki* (n. 65), 98; Belokurov, op. cit. (n. 67), 36; Massa, *Short History* (n. 64), 101; Brown, op. cit. (n. 21), 204; and Ivan Timofeev, *Vremennik*, ed. V. P. Adrianova-Peretts (M.-L., 1951), 490.

[84] Significantly, the author does not include Siberia among the territories under the supervision of the *Prikaz Kazanskogo Dvortsa*. This, coupled with the inclusion in his list of a Siberian *chetvert'* (see n. 89), would seem to indicate that, contrary to existing evidence, a separate administrative body for Siberia was already functioning by the end of the sixteenth century.

Ivan Narmanskoi,[85] and postnike demetroe ladiyin[86] the latter is clarke of the best border townes and castles[87] much imployed in the state, and overseeth the princes gold smythes paynters glaciers & such like[88]

Chetvert of Siberia[89] hath for diak Ivana Vofromeyevna[90] who dealeth with the revenewes and warres of the north east partes payeth the souldiares ther wages as the other diaks payethe gentrie in ther provences ||

Bolshoi prekhode [*Prikaz Bol'shogo Prikhoda*], or gret revenew receiveth the customes out of all cities and townes and the dewties out of all offices as alsoe out of the offices of the provences the overpluss of ther Tributes, giveth allowances to embassendors and strangers and payeth wages to such souldiers as the prince intertayneth. The Boyaren hereof is Knaze Ivan Vasilevich Sitskoye,[91] and the diaks Ondree Artsibashove[92] and Vasilie Nelowbove[93]

[85] Ivan Narmatsky served in the *Novyi Prikaz* in 1595–9. See Veselovsky, *D'yaki* (n. 65), 353–4; Brown, op. cit. (n. 21), 206.

[86] Postnik Dmitriev Lodygin was Narmatsky's colleague in the *Novyi Prikaz* in 1595–9. Before this appointment he served in the *Posol'skii Prikaz* (1589–92). Veselovsky, *D'yaki* (n. 65), 153; Belokurov, op. cit. (n. 67), 36; and Brown, op. cit. (n. 21), 206.

[87] 'best border townes and castles' is apparently a reference to north-western Russia, the administration of which was generally in the hands of the *Novyi Prikaz*. See Brown, op. cit. (n. 21), 177, 206, 589.

[88] The tsar's craftsmen were under the supervision of the *Oruzheinaya Palata*. It appears that the *d'yak* Lodygin oversaw this chancellery as well as the *Novyi Prikaz*. See S. K. Bogoyavlensky and G. A. Novitsky (eds.), *Gosudarstvennaya Oruzheinaya palata moskovskogo kremlya* (M., 1954), pp. iii, vi, viii.

[89] According to all evidence available hitherto, Siberia remained under the supervision of the *Prikaz Kazanskogo Dvortsa* until 1626, when the *Sibirskii Prikaz* was created. There is no reference, as far as is known, to a separate administrative body for Siberia before this date, but the existence of such a body by the end of the sixteenth century would not have been superfluous in view of the fact that it was precisely at this time that a considerable part of Siberia was steadily being brought under Russian control. It was during this period, moreover, that a number of fortresses were established along the main rivers and their tributaries to protect and control the growing number of Russian colonies in Siberia. Fletcher notes that a garrison of 6,000 Russian soldiers kept Siberia firmly under Muscovite control. See Fletcher, *Commonwealth* (n. 70), 63, 64; Brown, op. cit. (n. 21), 605; Kotoshikhin, *O Rossii* (n. 39), 93; and Raymond H. Fisher, *The Russian Fur Trade 1550–1700* (Berkeley, 1943), 36.

[90] This individual has not been identified. The possibility of a woman's holding such an office in the sixteenth century is so remote that there must be some doubt as to the accuracy of this entry.

[91] Prince Ivan Vasil'evich Sitsky, first mentioned in the court rank of *stol'nik* in 1577, was appointed boyar in 1585. In 1601, owing to his connections with the Romanovs, he fell into disgrace and was banished to a remote monastery, where he died in 1608. He cannot be traced in other sources to the *Bol'shoi Prikhod*. See Likhachev, *Razryadnye d'yaki* (n. 67), 167; Massa, *Short History* (n. 64), 35–6; Berry and Crummey, op. cit. (n. 43), 155; Novikov, op. cit. (n. 19), 61; Konrad Bussow, *Moskovskaya Khronika 1584–1613*, ed. I. I. Smirnov (M.-L., 1961), 345.

[92] Andrey Gavrilovich Artsybashev served as *d'yak* in the *Bol'shoi Prikhod* in 1577/8, and in 1598–1603. Before 1577 he was a *d'yak* in the *Razryadnyi Prikaz* and had also participated in diplomatic missions. He served for a while in the *Dvortsovyi Bol'shoi Prikhod* (1581–3) and in Novgorod (1586–91). He died probably in 1603. See Likhachev, *Razryadnye d'yaki* (n. 67), 472–3, 475; Veselovsky, *D'yaki* (n. 65), 33; *Russkii biograficheskii slovar'*, ii (1900), 340.

[93] Vasily Nelyubov Semenovich Sukov was a *d'yak* in the *Bol'shoi Prikhod* in 1598–1606. Before this he had been in the *Razboinyi Prikaz* (1584), the *Razryadnyi Prikaz* (1591/2–8), and in Novgorod and Kazan'. He remained a Moscow *d'yak* under the false Dmitry, and accompanied Afanasy Vlas'ev to Poland to meet Maryna Mniszek. Nelyubov found favour with Vasily Shuisky as well, but was removed when Shuisky fell. In 1610/11, however, he was summoned back to court by Sigismund of Poland. See Likhachev, *Razryadnye d'yaki* (n. 67), 474, 506; Veselovsky, *D'yaki* (n. 65), 500.

Strelskoi prikaze [*Streletskii Prikaz*] or ——[94] of 1500 gunners[95] hath for Boyaren Ivan Vasilivich Godonove,[96] and diaks Ivan Kapove[97] and Ignatie Safanove,[98] ther be 2 or three gholovas or captaines over 500 gunners appeece[99] as Levontie Ladivevosnie and postnike,[100] 500 || wach att on tyme, and if the Emp. ride abrode they have 500 horses out of his stables or more as the prince please to appointe[101] they receive yerelye five markes wages apeece a gowne cloth and certayne measures of graine[102]

Powshkarskoie prikaze [*Pushkarskii Prikaz*], or gret ordinance hath in the Boyarens place on Knaze Vasilie Semenovich Kostovkie,[103] and diakes Greghorie Klabownove,[104] and Ivan Timofeyeve[105] who see to the casting of gret ordinance and the making of smale shott and alsoe to the provision of copper powder and lead

Panskoie prikaze [*Panskii Prikaz*],[106] or office of souldiers that be polishe and

---

[94] The words 'gunners' and 'guard' are crossed out here.

[95] According to Hellie (*Enserfment* (n. 40), 203–5), the *strel'tsy* numbered some 20,000–25,000 by the end of the sixteenth century, 7,000–10,000 of whom were stationed in Moscow. Fletcher gives the number of Moscow *strel'tsy* as 5,000 (out of a total of 12,000). Margeret says they numbered 6,000. It is possible, however, that the figure in the manuscript pertains not to the total number of *strel'tsy* (whether in Moscow or at large), but to the number on duty in Moscow on any given day. The Kremlin was closely watched at all times by a *strel'tsy* guard of 500 (cf. the author's '500 wach att on tyme . . .'), which in shifts of three would amount to a total picket of 1,500. See Fletcher, *Commonwealth* (n. 70), 55; Margeret, op. cit. (n. 49), 73; and Zabelin, *Domashnii byt* (n. 44), 288.

[96] Ivan Vasil'evich Godunov was made a boyar in 1584. Other sources do not associate him with the *Streletskii Prikaz*. He died probably in 1602, although Massa claims that he survived his kinsman Boris Godunov, and was 'banished in the confines of Tatary'. See Massa, *Short History* (n. 64), 108; and Likhachev, *Razryadnye d'yaki* (n. 67), 20.

[97] Ivan Kapov has been identified as a *d'yak* in the *Streletskii Prikaz* in 1603/4. See Veselovsky, *D'yaki* (n. 65), 229.

[98] Ignaty Timofeevich Sofonov is first heard of in 1598 (as *d'yak* in the *Streletskii Prikaz*). The next mention of him here is in 1602. He turns up again in 1606 as a *d'yak* attending the false Dmitry's wedding. In 1611 he was serving as *voevoda* at Kaluga. See Likhachev, *Razryadnye d'yaki* (n. 67), 537; and Veselovsky, *D'yaki* (n. 65), 486.

[99] According to Hellie (*Enserfment* (n. 40), 163), during the sixteenth century a *strel'tsy* regiment (known as a *prikaz*) consisted of 500–1,000 men under the command of a single captain (*golova*). Margeret states that at the end of the sixteenth century a *strel'tsy* regiment contained only 500 men, a figure which is here confirmed by the author, although he places such a regiment under the command of more than one *golova*.

[100] These two individuals have not been identified.

[101] One of the Moscow *strel'tsy* regiments (the *stremennyi*) was indeed assigned to accompany the tsar on his travels. According to Fletcher (*Commonwealth* (n. 70), 56), this special requirement of horse guards numbered 2,000. See also Massa, *Short History* (n. 64), 73; and S. M. Solov'ev, *Istoriya Rossii s drevneishikh vremen* (M., 1959), 73.

[102] This confirms the statement of Margeret, who says (op. cit. (n. 49), 73) that the *strel'tsy* received 4 or 5 roubles and 12 *chetverti* of rye or oats. The cloth which they received came from the Royal Treasury. See also Solov'ev, *Istoriya* (n. 101), 74–5.

[103] This individual has not been identified.

[104] All that is known of Grigory Klobukov is that he was serving as *d'yak* in 1597/8, and was posted to the Novgorod *Razryad* in 1603/4. See Buganov, *Razryadnye knigi 1475–1598* (n. 75), 523; idem, *Razryadnye knigi 1559–1605* (n. 75), 351; and Likhachev, *Razryadnye d'yaki* (n. 67), 460.

[105] Ivan Kol Timofeev, the supposed author of the *Vremennik*, cannot be traced in other sources to the *Pushkarskii Prikaz*. He is, however, mentioned as a *d'yak* in connection with Grigory Klobukov in 1597/8. Later, he served at the *Bol'shoi Prikhod* (1605/5), Tula (1605/6 and 1607), Kaluga (1606/7), Novgorod (1607–9), Astrakhan' (1618–20), Yaroslavl' (1621–5), and Nizhnii Novgorod (1626–1627/8). See Likhachev, *Razryadnye d'yaki* (n. 67), 79; Veselovsky, *D'yaki* (n. 65), 514–15; Buganov, *Razryadnye knigi, 1475–1598* (n. 75), 523; and S. K. Bogoyavlensky, *Prikaznye sud'i XVII veka* (M.–L., 1946), 301.

[106] This is the earliest known reference to this *prikaz*; the next comes in 1614 (i.e. immediately

stranngers who receive ther charge and wages || ther cheife officer is Kneze Michailo Ghlebovich Saltikove[107] an Okolnichen, and Ignatie petrovich Tatischeve[108] a dvoranine of the counsell, the diake is Dorosei Bukhin,[109] the tow last have alsoe under them the

chelombuitnie prekaze [*Chelobitnyi Prikaz*] or office of requeste

Rozboie prikaze [*Razboinyi Prikaz*], for robberies hath for Boyaren Simon Nikitevich Romanove,[110] and diaks Ondree Totanine[111] and Timafei Petrove,[112] all traytors fellons murderes and robbers are sent from all places of the land ther to be tried punished and executed

Yamskoi prikaze [*Yamskoi Prikaz*], or post maisters office hath for cheife Yelezare Levontevich Rzhevskoie,[113] a dovoronine for || diake zakharie sviyazeve[114] they give post monye to such as ride upon the princes affaires and to embassendors and messengers, and see that the poste townes[115] be furnished with post horse and appointe newe post townes to anye place in the Emperors dominions placing the Emps. best

following the establishment of the Romanov dynasty). It is not surprising that this *prikaz* existed by the end of the sixteenth century in view of the considerable number of foreign mercenaries who entered Muscovite service during the reigns of Fedor Ivanovich (1584–98) and Boris Godunov (1598–1605) in order to shore up Russia's defences, which had proved to be inadequate when confronted by the armies of her western neighbours. The importance of the *Panskii Prikaz* is emphasized by the fact that it was headed by two members of the *duma*. See *Enserfment* (n. 40), 169–70; Brown, op. cit. (n. 21), 509; A. K. Baev, *Kurs istorii russkogo voennogo iskusstva*, i (Spb., 1900), 119; and Baron, 'Who Were the Gosti?' (n. 50), 3.

[107] Prince Mikhail Glebovich Saltykov was appointed *okol'nichii* in 1589/90 and boyar in 1601/2. After the death of Boris Godunov he became an energetic supporter of the false Dmitry and of the Poles. In 1610 he and other Muscovite notables arrived at the camp of Sigismund of Poland at Smolensk and offered him their services. Owing to his close connection with the Poles, Saltykov was in disgrace after the collapse of Muscovite support for a foreign tsar. In 1612 he chose self-imposed exile. He died in Poland. His involvement with the *Panskii Prikaz* (which is not attested in other sources) may explain how he came to develop strong ties with the Poles. See Likhachev, *Razryadnye d'yaki* (n. 67), 530, 539; Platonov, *Ocherki* (n. 64), 320; Bussow, *Moskovskaya Khronika* (n. 91), 165; N. Ikonnikov (ed.), *La Noblesse de Russie*, 2 ed. (Paris, 1958–66), xv. 193–4.

[108] A *dumnyi dvoryanin* since 1582, Ignaty Petrovich Tatishchev was appointed *kaznachei* in 1600, and *pechatnik* in 1601. He died in 1604. He is not otherwise known to have been linked to the *Chelobitnyi Prikaz*. See Ikonnikov, *Noblesse* (n. 107), xvii. 47; *Russkii biograficheskii slovar'*, xx. 351; and Berry and Crummey, op. cit. (n. 43), 156.

[109] Dorofey (Dorokha) Bokhin served as a *d'yak* in the *Razboinyi Prikaz* in 1584 and in the *Posol'skii Prikaz* in the capacity of *pristav* under the false Dmitry (1605/6). He cannot otherwise be traced to the *Chelobitnyi Prikaz*. See Buganov, *Razryadnye knigi 1475–1598* (n. 75), 413; and Veselovsky, *D'yaki* (n. 65), 67–8.

[110] This individual has not been identified.

[111] Andrey Tat'yanin is mentioned in the sources as a *d'yak* in 1597/8, but there is no indication as to where he was serving. See Buganov, *Razryadnye knigi 1475–1598* (n. 75), 458, 543.

[112] Timofey Petrov appears as *d'yak* in the sources (1588/9 and 1596–8), but there is no mention of his *prikaz*. See Veselovsky, *D'yaki* (n. 65), 412; and Buganov, *Razryadnye knigi 1475–1598* (n. 75), 516, 543.

[113] Elezary Leont'evich Rzhevsky was made a *dumnyi dvoryanin* in 1590 and died in 1599 as an *okol'nichii*. He is mentioned in the sources as a *d'yak* in 1596/7, but his *prikaz* is not named. See Buganov, *Razryadnye knigi 1475–1598* (n. 73), 250, 254, 297, 414, 515; Ikonnikov, *Noblesse* (n. 107), xiv. 33; *Russkii biograficheskii slovar'*, xvi. 156–7; and D. S. Likhachev, *Puteshestviya russkikh poslov XVI–XVII vv.* (M.–L., 1954), 364.

[114] Zakhary Grigor'ev Sviyazev was a *d'yak* in the *Yamskoi Prikaz* in 1596/7. Before this he served in the *Pomestnyi Prikaz*, *Kazanskii Dvor*, *Bol'shoi Dvorets*, and *Razryadnyi Prikaz*. In 1609 he was posted to the *Sudnyi Vladimirskii Prikaz*. See Likhachev, *Razryadnye d'yaki* (n. 67), 508–9; Buganov, *Razryadnye knigi 1475–1598* (n. 75), 339; and Bogoyavlensky, *Prikaznye sud'i* (n. 105), 294.

[115] The 'poste townes' were those areas, usually adjacent to a post station, where the *okhotniki*

husband men ther,[116] who paye noe rent for ther landes, save affording soe manye horse and receive iiid in monye for everie horse for Ten Mills[117]

Volodimerskoi prikaze [*Vladimirskaya Chet'/Vladimirskii Prikaz*], dealeth with the affaires of that dukedome the Boyaren is Kneze Nikita Romanovich Trobetskoi,[118] the diak Ivan Namaskoie[119]

demitrovskoi prikaze [*Sudnyi Dmitrovskii Prikaz*] || handelleth the contraversies betweene gentellmen the Boyaren is Knaze Vasilie Vasilivich Ghalitsin[120] the diakes Istoma yevskoi[121] and yurie Kondireve[122]

Razanskoi prikaze [*Sudnyi Ryazanskii Prikaz*], for the countrie of Razan the cheife is Knaze Ivan Vasilivech Velokogho ghaghin[123] an okolnichen the diake pilipe Solenischeve[124]

<hr>

(see n. 117), who ran the stations, lived. These areas were known as *yamskie slobody*. See I. Ya. Gurlyand, *Yamskaya gon'ba v moskovskom gosudarstve do kontsa XVII veka* (Yaroslavl', 1909), 154.

[116] Up to the mid sixteenth century the maintenance of post stations and the provision of carts and horses was the responsibility of the local population surrounding a station. Beginning in the 1550s, however, reforms were made which shifted this responsibility to a newly created group of officials known as *yamskie okhotniki*. These officials (the author's 'husband men') were chosen from among the more prosperous and hard-working peasants of a given locality and were assigned lands for their subsistence, usually near the station to which they were attached. See ibid. 122, 125, 131.

[117] Land held by the *okhotniki* was not taxed and they had no overlord to whom rent was owed. In fact, they rendered no other service to the state except that of operating the postal service. Those attached to the more important post stations received, until the end of the sixteenth century, about 10 *chetverti* of land (per field in a three-field system), while those assigned to lesser stations received about 5 *chetverti*. They also received money to help pay their travelling expenses. During the sixteenth century this came to about 3 *den'gi* for every 10 *versty* travelled, as confirmed here. See ibid. 124, 159.

[118] Prince Nikita Romanovich Trubetskoy was made a boyar between 1584 and 1586. He was one of Boris Godunov's most loyal supporters at the beginning of the Time of Troubles. He did, however, swear allegiance to the false Dmitry in 1606 and become a member of the latter's Great Council. He also found favour with Vasily Shuisky. He died probably in 1608. No other sources associate him with the *Vladimirskii Prikaz*. See Ikonnikov, *Noblesse* (n. 107), xviii. 384–5; Likhachev, *Razryadnye d'yaki* (n. 67), 167; and Berry and Crummey, op. cit. (n. 43), 154.

[119] On Ivan Narmatsky, cf. n. 85.

[120] He was prominent during the Time of Troubles. While on a campaign against the false Dmitry in 1605, he helped bring the Muscovite army over to the latter's side, and probably participated in the murder of Boris Godunov's widow and her son, the young tsar. For his co-operation he was awarded a seat in Dmitry's Great Council and the post of *dvoretskii*. He did not get along well with Dmitry's successor, Vasily Shuisky, and helped eventually to overthrow him. After Shuisky's ouster, Golitsyn accompanied Metropolitan Filaret to Poland in order to negotiate Władysław's assumption of the Russian throne. Both Golitsyn and Filaret were detained and interned at Marienburg until 1619. Golitsyn died at Wilno in 1619 on his way back to Moscow. He cannot be traced to the *Sudnyi Dmitrovskii Prikaz* in other sources. See Ikonnikov, *Noblesse* (n. 107), xv. 455, 456; Massa, *Short History* (n. 64), 74; Platonov, *Ocherki* (n. 64), 210, 213, 348.

[121] Istoma Evsky (or Evskoy) is mentioned in the sources as a *d'yak*, but his *prikaz* is not indicated (1578/9, 1584/5, and 1597/8). See Buganov, *Razryadnye knigi 1475–1598* (n. 75), 301, 357, 543.

[122] This individual has not been identified.

[123] Prince Ivan Vasil'evich Velikogo-Gagin (appointed *okol'nichii* in 1584) cannot be traced in other sources to the *Sudnyi Ryazanskii Prikaz*. See Novikov, op. cit. (n. 19), 61.

[124] Filipp Golenishchev (or Solenishchev) is mentioned as a *d'yak* in 1597/8, but his *prikaz* is not indicated. In 1602/3–1603/4 he was at the *Bol'shoi Prikhod*. See Buganov, *Razryadnye knigi 1475–1598* (n. 75), 516; and Bogoyavlensky, *Prikaznye sud'i* (n. 105), 245.

Kazenoi dvore [*Kazennyi Dvor*], or store howse the diakes be Ivan yenizinove[125] and Vasilie Tarakanove[126] thes men also be cheife of the Tamoshnoi dvore [*Tamozhennyi Prikaz*],[127] or custome howse, thes take into the princes storehowse clothes for liveries for the garde and such souldiers as desearve well in Siberia,[128] provide alsoe copper lead Tine wax honye cloth of gold silke carpette stuffes ffurres of all || sortes for the Emp. store, they seale weightes and measures appointe customers to send to cieties receive the marchante Bills of wares and take the cheife for the prince'giving money of exchanging wares take custome after the valewe of the wares and commande the marchante and cittizens to assist them to choose and valewe commodities for the Emp. use[129]

Zemskoi prikaze [*Zemskie Dvory/Zemskie Prikazy*], or guild for the cominalltye of the cittie[130] hath for Boyaren Greghorie Borrisovich Vasilchikov[131] and diaks Vasilie Shelipine[132] and Ivan Maximove,[133] this office is placed [illegible] without the Emp. castles gates wher are heard all the complainte of the cittizens and the offenderes severelye punished[134] ||

Kholopei prikaze [*Prikaz Kholop'ego Suda*], for bond servante hath for cheefe Mikhailo Ivanovich Vnowkove[135] and diake Mikhailo owinovskoie[136] wher all mens bond servant be inrolled with ther wives and children according to ther assurances[137]

Kaminoi prikaze [*Kamennyi Prikaz/Prikaz Kamennykh Del*] for stones and brikes for the princes building the diake is Nechai Perfileve[138]

[125] This individual has not been identified.

[126] Vasily Tarakanov was a *d'yak* at the *Kazennyi Dvor* in 1593, 1601/2, 1607, and 1609/10. See Veselovsky, *D'yaki* (n. 65), 506.

[127] This is the earliest known reference to this *prikaz*. The next is in 1604. See Brown, op. cit. (n. 21), 594; Demidova, 'Byurokratizatsiya' (n. 21), 216.

[128] On the vast array of fabrics held by the Royal Treasury for various purposes, see Solov'ev, *istoriya* (n. 101), 74–5; and Zabelin, *Domashnii byt* (n. 44), 377.

[129] The tsar was particularly interested in acquiring goods brought to Russia by foreign merchants. They were consequently at liberty to sell at large only after the officials of the Royal Treasury had inspected their goods and chosen on behalf of the tsar. The author implies that such goods as were purchased for the tsar were priced by some process of bargaining between the Treasury officials and the merchants. No doubt, however, the tsar must always have been *seen* to determine these prices himself. See Marc Szeftel, 'The Legal Condition of the Foreign Merchants in Muscovy', in: *Russian Institutions and Culture up to Peter the Great: Collected Essays*, ed. idem (London, 1975), 341.

[130] i.e. Moscow.

[131] Grigory Borisovich Vasil'chikov was at the *Zemskie Dvory* in 1597/8. It is not known when or whether he was made a boyar. See Buganov, *Razryadnye knigi 1475–1598* (n. 75), 334, 543.

[132] Vasily Shelepin served as a *d'yak* in 1585–7 and in 1597. Nothing more is known about him. See Veselovsky, *D'yaki* (n. 65), 587; and Buganov, *Razryadnye knigi 1475–1598* (n. 75), 378, 391.

[133] Maksimov was a *d'yak* at the *Razryadnyi Prikaz* in 1602 and at the *Bol'shoi Prikhod* in 1604/5–1605/6. Before this he was serving in Moscow, but it is not known where. See Veselovsky, *D'yaki* (n. 65), 312; Buganov, *Razryadnye knigi 1475–1598* (n. 75), 543; Bogoyavlensky, *Prikaznye sud'i* (n. 105), 272.

[134] The 1550 *Sudebnik* provided considerably harsher punishments than those established by the earlier Law Code (1497). See H. W. Dewey. 'The 1550 *Sudebnik* as an Instrument of Reform', *Jahrbücher für Geschichte Osteuropas*, NS x (1962), 166.

[135] This individual has not been identified.

[136] Mikhail Unkovsky was a *d'yak* in 1597–1600, and in 1604/5. Nothing more is known about him. See Veselovsky, *D'yaki* (n. 65), 533; Buganov, *Razryadnye knigi 1475–1598* (n. 75), 543.

[137] By 'assurances' the author means the legal documents (*gramoty*) which spelled out the nature of an individual's slave status.

[138] Nechay Fedorovich Perfil'ev was a *d'yak* at Moscow in 1599/1600 and at the *Pushkarskii Prikaz* in 1613, but he has not otherwise been traced to the *Kamennyi Prikaz*. See Veselovsky, *D'yaki* (n. 65), 406; and Bogoyavlensky, *Prikaznye sud'i* (n. 105), 284.

Zhitnishnoi dvorets [*Zhitnyi Dvor/Zhitnyi Prikaz*], or corne howse looketh to the provision of meale for the princes howse the diak is zakharie yupeneve[139]

Kazanskoie chetvert [*Sudnyi Kazanskii Prikaz*] hath for his diake Semeika Sowmarakove[140] he dealeth for all matters in the countrie of Kazan.

---

[139] This individual has not been identified.

[140] Semen (Semeika) Sumorokov served as a *d'yak* in several *prikazy*, including the *Bol'shoi Prikhod* (1582), *Chetvertnyi Prikaz* and the *Ustyuzhnaya Chet'* (1582, 1591–8), and the *Yamskoi Prikaz* (1587). He cannot, however, be traced to the *Sudnyi Kazanskii Prikaz* in other sources. See Veselovsky, *D'yaki* (n. 65), 501–2; Buganov, *Razryadnye knigi 1475–1598* (n. 75), 364, 379, 515, 543; and Brown, op. cit. (n. 21), 205.

The Folklore Origins of Mickiewicz's *Dziady*: Olimpia Swianiewiczowa's Interpretation

By NINA TAYLOR

1

In his Introduction to *Dziady* (Parts 2 and 4) (1823) Mickiewicz asserts that the *dziady* ceremony has been known to all pagan peoples since pre-Christian times.[1] Once known as the feast of the ram, it has been amalgamated with concepts of the Christian religion and with All Souls' Day (2 November). It is held, he says, in many districts of Lithuania, Prussia, and Livonia to honour the memory of dead forebears. The Koźlarz, Huslar, or Guślarz (a combination of magician, soothsayer, priest, and poet) officiates. The clergy and landowners, Mickiewicz tells us, are endeavouring to eradicate the custom, owing to its connection with superstitious practices and 'often reprehensible excesses'. The ceremony is celebrated 'in chapels or deserted houses near cemeteries', and includes a banquet consisting of various victuals, liquors, and fruits. The ghosts of the dead are summoned, it being assumed that food and drink will bring relief to souls in purgatory. On an apparently autobiographical note, Mickiewicz continues:

The pious intent of the feast, the solitary localities, the nocturnal hour, the fantastic rituals once appealed strongly to my imagination. I heard fables, tales, and songs about dead men returning with requests or warnings. In all these monstrous inventions one might perceive certain moral aspirations and teachings . . .[2]

It is not known whether Mickiewicz attended the *dziady* ceremony in the Uniate church in Cyryn,[3] in the small Uniate chapel on the top of a

---

[1] Adam Mickiewicz, *Dzieła*, iii (Warsaw, 1949), 11. Cf. J. Kallenbach, 'Tło. obrzędowe *Dziadów*' in: idem, *Czasy i ludzie* (Warsaw, 1905), 87–133.

[2] Mickiewicz, loc. cit.

[3] This location is favoured by Leonard Podhorski-Okołów. The annexe to a plan of Cyryn dated 1817 (he says) shows part of the meadow as 'an area of ground with burial-mounds' and 'ancient tombstones' adjacent to the church. An Orthodox church and belfry were built there in 1857 in place of the Uniate buildings of Mickiewicz's time, and an Orthodox vicarage replaced the house of the Uniate priest at the foot of the church hill. In 1937 it was still 'covered in numerous tombstones' and had 'a fairly typical lay-out for the province of Nowogródek', with its long row of huts and small houses along the right edge of the Serwecz valley. See L. Podhorski-Okołów, *Realia mickiewiczowskie*, i (Warsaw, 1952), 134–40.

hill in the park at Tuhanowicze,[4] or in Zapole,[5] but the experience must have preceded his admission to the University of Wilno (1817), judging by the fact that it is not referred to in the correspondence of the Philomaths.[6] It has been suggested that Mickiewicz attended *dziady* in his school-days in the company of his friend Jan Czeczot, from whose knowledge of local folk culture he was more than once to benefit, and who had been baptized in the Uniate parish church of Worończa (Korelicze), five miles to the south of his native village of Małuszyce.[7] The event may have occurred in 1812, the year of Mickiewicz's father's death, when in the aftermath of Napoleon's retreat from Moscow the countryside of Nowogródek was impregnated with death and the celebration of *dziady* must have been particularly awesome.[8] Some scholars, however, have warned against taking Mickiewicz's declarations at face value, claiming that he probably never attended the *dziady* ceremony at all and that his inspiration was literary in origin.[9]

2

There exists a fairly substantial number of texts describing what may be a prototype of the *dziady* ceremony. The earliest description of the Old Prussian and Old Lithuanian feast of the ram, consisting of a sermon on ancestral deeds followed by an animal sacrifice, confession, absolution, and much inebriated shouting, is by Simon Grünau, a German Dominican from Gdańsk.[10] There can be no doubt that Mickiewicz knew this text, as well as other accounts of the ceremony. He had spent part of the autumn of 1822 browsing in the well-stocked library of the Chreptowicz family estate at Szczorsy[11] and doing

[4] See J. M. Rymkiewicz, *Żmut* (Paris, 1987), 185.   [5] Ibid. 253.

[6] J. Czubek (ed.), *Archiwum Filomatów, Część I: Korespondencja 1815–1823* (Cracow, 1913). Mention is, however, made of a student feast held in a barn or threshing-floor near Wilno on Low Sunday, 17 April 1821, when Mickiewicz's friends celebrated their communal Easter in ritualized ribaldry. See ibid., *Część III: Poezja Filomatów* (Cracow, 1922), ii. 348.

[7] See A. B. McMillin, 'Jan Čačot in Byelorussian and Polish Literature', *The Journal of Byelorussian Studies*, ii (1969), 57–68.

[8] See e.g. Jan Czeczot, 'Duma nad mogiłami Francuzów, roku 1813 za Wilnem przy drodze, do Nowogródka prowadzącej, pogrzebanych', in Czubek, *Archiwum, Część III* (n. 6), 9–20, and the description of Wilno after the passage of the *Grande Armée* in Aleksander Fredro, *Trzy po trzy: Pamiętniki* (Cracow, 1949), 45–6.

[9] A. Brückner, *Literatura polska*, ed. S. Lam, 2 ed. (Paris, 1947), 153.

[10] See St. Pigoń, *Do źródeł 'Dziadów' kowieńsko-wileńskich* (Wilno, 1930), 80–5. Grünau's *Preussische Chronik* (written *c.*1510) was summarized and commented on by Lukas David, whose own *Preussische Chronik* (written in 1576) was published in Königsberg in 1812. David's Chronicle was in turn used almost verbatim by Maciej Stryjkowski in his *Kronika polska, litewska, żmodzka i wszystkiej Rusi* (Königsberg, 1582) and by A. Kotzebue in *Preussens aeltere Geschichte* (Riga, 1809). Mickiewicz had read all these accounts (Grünau, David, Stryjkowski, and Kotzebue).

[11] M. Dernałowicz, Ks. Kostenicz, and Z. Makowiecka, *Kronika życia i twórczości Mickiewicza: lata 1798–1824* (Warsaw, 1957), 340–1. On Szczorsy, see R. Aftanazy, *Materiały do dziejów rezydencji*, iia (Warsaw, 1986), 446–59.

preliminary work on *Grażyna*, which was published in the same
volume as *Dziady* (Parts 2 and 4). From his footnotes to *Grażyna* it is
apparent that he had consulted all the major sixteenth-century Polish
chronicles, as well as certain later publications such as Tadeusz
Czacki's *O litewskich i polskich prawach* (Warsaw, 1800–1).

Another relevant text of which Mickiewicz was undoubtedly aware is
Maria Czarnowska's description of *radawnica*,[12] a springtime festival in
honour of dead ancestors, celebrated in Hrubieńszczyzna on the River
Wołcza, a tributary of the Soż. Held on the Tuesday afternoon following Low Sunday, it comprised egg-rolling, alms-giving, and libations to
the dead, who were invited to join in a picnic-like feast beside the
village tombstones. It usually ended in revelry and dancing at the local
tavern. Czarnowski's account was published in the *Dziennik Wileński*
while Mickiewicz was still studying at the University in Wilno. It
stimulated such interest that Teodor Łoziński was shortly afterwards
invited to read a paper[13] to a meeting of the Philomath Society concerning peasant traditions in his native village of Zabrudzie in Volhynia. Of
course, Mickiewicz's familiarity with printed sources does not preclude
the possibility of his having had first-hand experience of the rite, but
the written sources may have first revealed to him the latent dramatic
tensions and scenic potential of the *dziady* ceremony.

3

Dziady has engendered a considerable body of critical literature,[14]
sometimes fanciful, often conflicting. Yet the problem of the drama's
folkloric prototype has persistently caused confusion and remains
largely unresolved.[15] Many genetic and interpretational inconsistencies
have been clarified by the first-hand experience and analysis, as yet
unpublished, of Olimpia Swianiewiczowa, née Zambrzycka, whose
lifelong dissatisfaction with the canon of *Dziady* criticism prompted her
a few years before her death to put together her own recollections and

[12] Maria Czarnowska, 'Zabytki mitologii słowiańskiej w zwyczajach wiejskiego ludu na Białej
Rusi dochowywane', *Dziennik Wileński*, vi (1817), 400–3. Abridged in L. Gołębiowski, *Lud polski:
jego zwyczaje, zabobony* [. . .] (Warsaw, 1830; repr. Warsaw, 1983), 268–70, and in Oskar Kolberg,
Dzieła wszystkie, lii. *Białoruś-Polesie* (Warsaw, 1968), 101–2.
[13] Entitled 'O niektórych obrzędach pospólstwa w okolicach Żytomierza'. See St. Pigoń,
'Wołyńskie przewody—wiosenne święto zmarłych', in: idem, *Drzewiej i wczoraj: wokół zagadnień
kultury i literatury* (Cracow, 1966), 61–75.
[14] Two of the most interesting recent studies are M. Masłowski, 'La Structure initiatique des
Aïeux (Dziady) d'Adam Mickiewicz', *Revue des études slaves*, lvii (1985), 421–45, and R. Przybylski,
'Epifanie Bohatera Polaków (1)', *Res Publica*, i (1987), no. 4, pp. 65–80, and no. 5, pp. 29–42
(extracts from a forthcoming book).
[15] See J. Krzyżanowski (ed.), *Słownik folkloru polskiego* (Warsaw, 1965), 93. There is a detailed
analysis by Maria Wantowska, '*Dziady* kowieńsko-wileńskie', in: J. Krzyżanowski and
R. Wojciechowski (eds.), *Ludowość u Mickiewicza* (Warsaw, 1958), 290–1.

inferences on the subject. These survive in an unpublished manuscript bearing her name and the title 'Interpretacja *Dziadów* Mickiewicz-owskich na podstawie skarbca kultury białoruskiej'.[16] In the main, Swianiewiczowa reproaches Mickiewicz scholars for their ignorance both of historical background and of local *realia* and lore. The conclusions she reaches amount to a total reversal of the received opinion exemplified in the work of Pigoń and others. As her contribution is rooted in specific topographical and cultural *realia*, it will first be necessary to outline the geographic and historical context of her life and work.

In about 1807 Olimpia's great-grandfather, Walenty Zambrzycki (died 1831), son of Józef, left his native *guberniya* of Mohylew. Some 35 km. to the West of Minsk, 15 km. from Zasław, 8 km. from Radoszkowicze (where the nearest market was to be found), and a couple of kilometres from the source of the River Wiazyńka (a tributary of the Udranka which, via the Ilia and the Wilia, joins it to the river network of the Niemen), he bought the two estates of Hurnowicze and Wiazyń together with the interlying village of Sieledczyki.[17] It was at this point that the Polish–Soviet frontier established by the Treaty of Riga (1921) later intersected the Mołodeczno–Minsk railway-line. From Sieledczyki to nearby Olechnowice (12 km. away by the road), a short cut could be taken through the Forest of Dekszniany, where in Olimpia's childhood a notorious spot called Wisielica ('Hangman's Nook'), at the junction of the Dekszniany and Dziublewska roads, was held in dread by the local inhabitants.[18] The neighbourhood is described as being hilly and fairly wooded, and having a clayey soil.[19]

In Wiazyń (sometimes known as Wiazyńka to distinguish it from the Wiazyń of the Gicewicz family in the district of Wilejka and the Wiazyń of the Bohdaszewskis near Kojdania) Walenty built a manor-house. On the right bank of the Wiazyńka, on a terrace above the level of spring floods opposite a ford, between the village of Sieledczyki and the estate outbuildings, he demarcated a cemetery to serve the needs of the three neighbouring villages of Sieledczyki, Hurnowicze, and Lipienie, located on the river's left bank, and had a small Uniate church built and consecrated to St George. Both tombs and church could be seen

---

[16] It consists of 162 folios of typescript and 31 folios of handwritten notes, numbered on one side. Archives of the Polish Institute and Sikorski Museum in London (hereafter PISM), shelf-mark KOL 261. Subsequent references will be to 'Interpretacja'. I am grateful to the Institute for giving permission to quote. In the passages and terms quoted from Swianiewiczowa's typescript and manuscripts her unorthodox Belorussian spelling is retained.

[17] O. Swianiewiczowa, 'Pogrzeby, stypy i dziady we wsi Sieledczyki', *Rocznik Polskiego Towarzystwa Naukowego na Obczyźnie*, x (1959–60), 80–8.

[18] 'Interpretacja', 62.

[19] *Słownik geograficzny Królestwa Polskiego i innych krajów słowiańskich*, ed. B. Chlebowski, xiii (Warsaw, 1893), 277.

from the manor-house windows.[20] Country folk would come from far and wide to attend the fair held here on 23 April. On major feast-days mass was celebrated here by the Uniate parish priest from Zasław, whither the villagers betook themselves for christenings and weddings. Funerals, however, were held *in situ*, and until the day of the burial the corpse was kept in the church, where it was customary to chant the praise of the deceased. The entire population of Sieledczyki was Uniate until 1865, when the parish of Zasław and the last Uniate church on the Wiazyń estate were finally abolished, having miraculously escaped that same fate two and a half decades earlier.

Though representing the Polish tradition in these parts (Olimpia's maternal grandfather, Alojzy Witkowski, was in the Insurrection of 1863, while her aunt, Wiktoria Bobrowska, was an indomitable organizer of clandestine Polish-language teaching, intervening with the Russian authorities when the young teachers under her care were indicted), the Zambrzycki family had close ties with the ambient Belorussian culture. Olimpia's grandfather Stanisław (1823–1907), a genial, artless rhymer, wrote occasional verses in both Polish and Belorussian.[21] As a collector of local folklore he was particularly interested in the structure of burial-mounds, his research in this field being inspired by the endeavours of Adam Kirkor and Eustachy Tyszkiewicz.[22] The father of the Belorussian poet Janka Kupala (real name Yan Lutsevich) leased a farm belonging to the Wiazyń estate,[23] and according to Zambrzycki family tradition, the poet learned to read and write at the manor.[24] Before the First World War Kupala's future wife, Władysława, was involved in the clandestine teaching of Polish, of which she had a perfect command.[25] The friendship between the Zambrzycki and Lutsevich families spanned several generations.

[20] O. Swianiewiczowa's letter to St. Pigoń, dated 29 Nov. 1965. This is one of four letters from Swianiewiczowa to Pigoń now deposited at the Jagellonian Library in Cracow (shelf-mark Przyb. 281/76). I am grateful to Professor Pigoń's family for granting me permission to obtain a microfilm of them. A summary of the correspondence was published by Swianiewiczowa in 'Spór o ludowy pierwowzór *Dziadów*', *Wiadomości*, no. 22 (1471), 9 June 1974, p. 1.

[21] A manuscript of his work is still in the possession of Olimpia's family. His poem 'Hutarka Staliuka' (1870–90) is mentioned in *Yanka Kupala: Entsyklapedychny davednik* (Minsk, 1986), 239.

[22] Ibid. Cf. '"Ostatni obywatel Wielkiego Księstwa Litewskiego": ze Stanisławem Swianiewiczem rozmawia Marek J. Karp', *Res Publica*, i (1987), no. 6, pp. 33–41.

[23] This was apparently between 1880 and 1883, when the tenancy expired (*Yanka Kupala* (n. 21), 137). Janka Kupala left Wiazyń in 1887 (ibid. 703).

[24] Letter from Stanisław Swianiewicz to Nina Taylor dated 28 June 1987. A. B. McMillin, *A History of Byelorussian Literature from its Origins to the Present Day* (Giessen, 1977), 175ff., alludes to Kupala's 'peripatetic' childhood between Wilejka and Minsk, and his use of Zygmunt Czachowicz's large private library at Sieliszcze. This is apparently substantiated by a reference in Kupala's autobiography (*Yanka Kupala* (n. 21), 703).

[25] The entry in *Yanka Kupala* (n. 21), 361–2, stresses her political radicalism.

4

Olimpia exemplifies the family's close involvement with Belorussian culture. She was born in Homel on 19 November 1902 (Old Style),[26] and apart from three years at the *pension* of Mrs Wołoska in Warsaw (1911–14) and a spell (after 1915) in the Polish gymnasium in Minsk, she spent most of her childhood on the family estate of Wiazyń, of which her father had taken over the management in 1906. Like many of the manor-houses in the vicinity, Wiazyń offered hospitality to wandering beggars, men and women who had escaped forcible conversion to Orthodoxy following the suppression of the Uniate Church in 1839 and the reprisals against the Roman Catholic Church after 1863, and who went on pilgrimages to the holy places of Ostra Brama in Wilno and Kalwaria nearby, thereby eschewing the attention of the tsarist police. These pilgrims brought political news from the world at large and, during the winter months, were given shelter in the villages and yeoman-farmsteads in return for teaching the children of the house their catechism. Olimpia recalls one such beggar who visited Wiazyń every year until the outbreak of the First World War, invariably bringing 'patriotic' news[27] concerning the prospects of Poland's emancipation from Russia.

From an early age, Olimpia took part in the daily life of the Belorussian village, feeding the swine with the village girls, driving the horses during the corn-threshing.[28] With parental blessing, moreover, she was the constant companion and self-appointed 'assistant' to the Sieledczyki village swineherd, the orphan Bazyli Szarenda, who entertained her with numerous tales of local legend and lore that he had heard from his uncle Iljuk Szarenda. These included intimate details of *dziady* celebrations held in the past, in the course of which her grandmother's misdemeanours had been revealed.[29] From another member of the same family, Hanka Szarenda, Olimpia learned a song that is relevant to the folkloric background of *Dziady*:

[26] The obituary by M. Znamierowska-Prufferowa in *Lud*, lx (1976), 381–3, is based on information which had been acquired from Swianiewiczowa herself. It also contains a bibliography.

[27] Letter to Pigoń dated 29 Nov. 1965 (n. 20). One of Stanisław Zambrzycki's poems, entitled 'Karta', tells the story of a beggar who escaped persecution after 1863. Swianiewiczowa here suggests an analogy with E. Tyszkiewicz, *Wilia i jej brzegi* (Dresden, 1871), 161–8.

[28] These details are recorded in an unpaginated manuscript notebook by Swianiewiczowa entitled 'Pamiętnik z pobytu w Indonezji' (PISM, shelf-mark KOL 261).

[29] 'Interpretacja', 4–6. Stanisław Swianiewicz's letter to Nina Taylor dated 28 June 1987 mentions how as a small girl Olimpia was befriended by an old shepherd named Szarenda, to whom she owed much of her intellectual and spiritual upbringing.

Wiasna

Byŭ u baćki adzin syn
Ale jon baćki nia słuchaŭ
Uziaŭ i na wajnu pajechaŭ

A tam jamu Boh nie pamoh
Jaho konik haroj loh
A siadzielca kamieniam
A sam mołod jaworam

Praz toj jawor ścieżeczka
Tudoj iszła dziewaczka
Rusoju kosu czesała
S jaworam razmaulała

Jak ty ciapier zialon, charosz
Budzia tabie luty maroz
Twaje pierja pamierznuć
Twaje wićja pasochnuć.

Oj! dziauczynka, dziauczynka
Jak ty ciapier u mamki
Tak ty ciapier małada i charasza

Ale budzia tabie lichi muż
Twaich pleczak nadabje
Twaich kosak nadarwie.

Badaj ty jaworu nie dażdaŭ
Jak ty mnie harda atkazaŭ.[30]

From childhood Olimpia was thus familiar with local peasant
customs, including the rituals connected with death, funerals, and the
cult of the departed. When the death throes began, a candle that had
been blessed on Candlemas Day was lit, and the round iron door in the
stove was opened to facilitate the exit of the sinful human soul.[31] In the
case of prolonged agony a hole was made in the ceiling for the same
purpose. News of the death would be passed on to the bees and the
horses, or in the case of a deceased woman, to the cows, sheep, pigs,
and poultry. Various auguries could then be based on the position of
the dead person's eyes. The corpse was elegantly attired, complete with
hat, 'so that he can bow to God', and some favourite object, together
with a few coins of 'ransom' money, was placed inside the coffin, which
was made with the help of neighbours.[32]

---

[30] 'Interpretacja', 59–60.   [31] Swianiewiczowa, 'Pogrzeby' (n. 17), 83.
[32] Ibid. Another custom is mentioned in a letter from Swianiewiczowa to Pigoń (n. 20) of
11 May 1968: when Jazepicha (Jazep's wife) died, every woman in the village brought an offering
of victuals that were placed at the head of the coffin and were not covered by a cloth, so that
Jazepicha, who had been hospitable all her life, could see who had brought what.

Hałasilnice, professional wailers, then came to pray and sing religious chants. On these occasions the prayers, likewise the litany for the souls of the dead, were *always* recited in Polish.[33] As only the innocent could escort the departed on their way to the cemetery, the coffin, after bidding farewell to the homestead, was led on its last road by a child aged between three and five. All present at the burial were invited to the funeral banquet where, again, only Polish prayers were said, the Angelus and Eternal Rest being the most popular. During the feast the nearest of kin circulated among the guests, relating to each in turn, sometimes in rhymed form, incidents from the deceased's life (*pryhowory*) that stimulated village gossip for months to come. Six weeks later a second banquet was held.[34]

5

In the Sieledczyki calendar, the *dziady* ceremony remained the most significant manifestation of peasant death lore, having been 'preserved until this day in all but its purest form'.[35] Conversations with the village women enabled Swianiewiczowa to ascertain that in those parts of Belorussia where the Uniate Church prevailed, seven days in the liturgical year had formerly been consecrated to the cult of the dead. By the beginning of the twentieth century, however, these rituals survived only fragmentarily.[36]

Known as 'holy evenings', the entire Christmas holiday from 24 December to 6 January was a period of communion with the dead. According to an established formula their souls were invited on three occasions to partake of a communal family supper consisting of specially prepared *kutia* (pearl barley): *kutia postnaya* (fasting *kutia*) on Christmas Eve before the Advent fast was broken, *kutia bohataya* (rich *kutia*) on New Year's Eve, when household supplies were abundant, and *biednaya kutia* (poor *kutia*) on the eve of the Feast of the Epiphany, when provisions were running out. After supper, prayers were said for the souls of the dead, and the gift of divination was then granted until midnight.[37]

---

[33] Swianiewiczowa, 'Pogrzeby' (n. 17), 84. In 'Spór' (n. 20) Swianiewiczowa states specifically that the Angelus was said at *dziady* ceremonies and at funerals 'if no Orthodox priest was present'.

[34] Swianiewiczowa, 'Pogrzeby' (n. 17), 85.

[35] Swianiewiczowa's notebook entitled 'Katakumby unitów białoruskich' (PISM, shelf-mark KOL 261), fol. 29.

[36] O. Swianiewiczowa, 'Dziady białoruskie', *Rocznik Polskiego Towarzystwa Naukowego na Obczyźnie*, xi (1960–1), 87.

[37] Ibid. 88–9. See also O. Swianiewiczowa, 'The Byelorussian Feast of the Dead' [translated from the Polish by Mrs Halina Bohdanowicz, to whom I am grateful for giving me a photocopy], *Sift*, 1974 no. 2, pp. 40–7 (hereafter referred to as *Sift*). For a Belorussian account of *dziady*, see Adam Varlyga, *Chatyry urachystas'tsi* (New York, 1970), 50–3.

Numerous taboos were in force during this period. There was to be no leavening of bread, no baking, no cleaning of stoves and chimneys, no slaughtering of livestock, no darning (as the sheep would be spotted and their wool thus no good for weaving), and no spinning (for 'what is spun on a holy evening is suitable only for the devil's pants').[38] No hard work should be started, though it was permitted to begin a job that could be finished on the same day, and to finish a job that had already been started. The ancestral spirits would take moderate vengeance for small trespasses, but failure to celebrate their feast could entail grave consequences for the offender, such as hailstones, cattle plague, and crop pestilence.[39] Though Roman Catholics, the Zambrzyckis incorporated a modified version of the winter *dziady* into their celebration of Christmas: during the 'holy evenings' prayers were said both before and after supper for the souls of the departed, who were not, however, invited to partake of the meal.[40]

In the spring there were three ceremonies in honour of the dead. On the Tuesday after Easter a more solemn supper than usual was held: food and liquor were set aside for the dead, and not cleared away at the end of the meal. On the same day it was customary for bereaved mothers singly and discreetly to place eggs (*kraszanki*) on their children's graves. Swianiewiczowa accordingly terms this ritual 'children's *dziady*'.[41] The traditional Whit Monday invitation to the spirits of the departed had almost totally vanished even before the First World War. By the time of Olimpia's childhood all that survived of the ritual was a general taboo on music and dancing on this day. On St John's Eve, Olimpia and her sister would wash in wheat dew, then, without talking, go quickly to bed to be sure of having a prophetic dream. Banned for years by the Orthodox clergy and police alike, the Midsummer's Eve bonfire was restored by Olimpia's father in 1912 on the hill known as 'Ararat' and attended by the inhabitants of Sieledczyki, Lipienie, and Krynica. The following year, the village of Girewicze at the foot of the highest hill in the Minsk morainic ridge (356 m.), some 5 km. as the crow flies from 'Ararat', followed suit.[42] The feast was characterized by the cult of animals (food was thrown under the

---

[38] *Sift*, 44.

[39] Swianiewiczowa, 'Dziady białoruskie' (n. 36), 90.

[40] Swianiewiczowa, 'Pamiętnik' (n. 28). Swianiewiczowa also adduces the testimony of Seweryn Wysłouch, from the estate of Pirkowicze in the district of Drohiczyn in Polesie, where Christmas Eve was a day of communication with dead ancestors. The family graves in the park near the palace were visited, and a consecrated wafer left on each grave. 'Interpretacja', 105–6.

[41] 'Dziady dzieci i młodzieży'. See 'Interpretacja', 127–8. In a letter to Pigoń dated 20 Oct. 1965 (n. 20) Swianiewiczowa describes other Easter traditions, such as the singing of 'Mały żak' on Easter Sunday, in which she often took part with other children, and the custom of the *wołoczebnicy*, who went round the cottages on Easter Monday collecting gifts of bacon and sausage.

[42] 'Interpretacja', 110–11. Swianiewiczowa also gives the texts of songs connected with St John's Eve, ibid. 107–8.

table at supper-time, in the belief that an understanding of animal and vegetable speech would be granted this night), contact with witches, interference of evil spirits in human affairs, and communion with the dead 'not only at the feast, but in solitude at night in the forest or cemetery'.[43]

6

The focal point of ancestor cult, however, was the autumn *dziady*, celebrated on a day chosen by each individual village within a three-week period starting the week before and ending two weeks after the feast of St Demetrius the Martyr (26 October), or 'emperor Demetrius' (*cesarz Dmitryj*) as he was known to the peasantry.[44] Only the foolhardy would visit the nearby Forest of Dekszniany and 'Hangman's Nook' during the 'Demetrius *dziady*', as the ghosts of those who had committed suicide were wont to roam the world at this time.[45] Indoors, meanwhile, a supper was held and special dishes served. The most important part of the ceremony, after which eating began, was the ritual invitation to the souls of the dead to partake communally of the supper.

In Swianiewiczowa's childhood *dziady* was always celebrated within the intimacy of the peasant cottages; it was restricted to localities belonging to the former *guberniya* of Minsk, and was not to be found in the Wilno area. Stanisław Swianiewicz recalls attending the celebration of *dziady* in the first autumn after his marriage to Olimpia.[46] No lamps or candles were used. The only light came from the stove and the doors were left open so that the spirits could enter with ease. Swianiewiczowa has left a detailed account:

To emphasize the fact that all the courses have been prepared from home produce, a soup made with the head of a slaughtered animal, together with the boiled head, must be on the table throughout the feast. The ritual food ensures that the forefathers can have no doubts about the offering which is made in their honour.

The feast commences with an invitation to the dead souls to partake of it. When all the guests have been gathered at the table, the host, or

[43] 'Interpretacja', 108; *Sift*, 46.

[44] Swianiewiczowa, 'Interpretacja', 64, quotes P. V. Shein, *Materialy dlya izucheniya byta i yazyka russkogo naseleniya severno-zapadnogo kraya, sobrannye i privedennye v poryadok* [. . .] (Spb., 1890), vol. i, pt. 2, p. 602. *Dmitrievskaya subbota*, introduced by Dmitry Donskoy to commemorate those who died at the Battle of Kulikovo and celebrated on the Saturday before the feast of St Demetrius, is a specifically Russian and Orthodox celebration.

[45] 'Interpretacja', 62.

[46] Letter from St. Swianiewicz to Nina Taylor dated 28 June 1987. Cf. Karp, '"Ostatni obywatel"' (n. 22), 37.

the hostess, pronounces the following formula: 'All the souls of the dead, we invite you to take your place at the table with us.'[47]

When these words have been said, the hostess pours a few spoonfuls of the soup made from the animal's head into a bowl, then adds a few pieces of meat and small portions from the other dishes. After this, she invites all those present to take their seats. The feast starts with a toast to the dead. Each guest pours a few drops from his glass on to the table-cloth, also for the dead. During the feast the dead are the topic of the conversation; and in the conversation all their good and bad character-istics are discussed, as well as the grievous experiences of their lives. The memories of the dead are not limited to the relatives; all the more important personalities of the neighbourhood must also be remem-bered.[48]

Swianiewiczowa has also recorded the impressions of one Franciszek Kućko-Żukowski, who was invited by Bazyli Hryszkiewicz of the once Uniate, now Orthodox, parish of Krasna (commune of Bielica, district of Lida) to attend the *dziady* ceremony 'on a Monday at the end of October or beginning of November'. The table was laid with a cloth and set with food. Bazyli lit a candle blessed at Candlemas, held it over the crocks three times, then opened the window, made the sign of the cross and said:

> Światyje dziady chodzicie siudy
> Macie jeści i pici,
> Tolka proszu, krywdy nam nie rabici.

After which all fell to. After eating, those present all knelt and recited the Angelus together. The food was not cleared from the table, and the window was left open all night. Next morning all the members of the household came to the table where the crocks were, but the food was reheated. After breakfast Bazyli lit the candle, passed it three times over the crocks, handed the lit candle to his wife, raised his hand in a move-ment of thrusting away and repeated three times, 'Światyje dziady, mieliście szto jeści i pici a ciapier idzicia', whereupon his wife extin-guished the candle and all present knelt and said the Angelus.[49]

Although in Swianiewiczowa's experience the *dziady* ceremony was always celebrated indoors, she adduces evidence to the contrary of one Julia Lisowska, née Tomaszewicz, from the estate of Dmitrowszczyzna

[47] The Polish version of the formula (see Swianiewiczowa, 'Dziady białoruskie' (n. 36), 88) is: 'Wszystkie dusze zmarłe, prosim was, abyście zasiadły z nami do wspólnej wieczerzy.'

[48] *Sift*, 41–2.

[49] Letter from Swianiewiczowa to Pigoń dated 29 Nov. 1965 (n. 20). In the 1930s Swianiewiczowa informed St. Stankiewicz that in Sieledczyki cold dishes were prepared for the living, and hot for the dead 'as the spirits are nourished by the steam'. See St. Stankiewicz, *Pier-wiastki białoruskie w polskiej poezji romantycznej: część I (do roku 1830)* (Wilno, 1936), 176–226.

in the district of Lepel (*guberniya* of Witebsk).[50] As a child (apparently in the 1890s) Lisowska had participated in a *dziady* ceremony secretly celebrated at full moon in the cemetery of nearby Bobynicze,[51] whose Uniate church had recently been made Orthodox. In the evening villagers went singly to the burial-ground. Each brought his own spoon and an offering of milk, honey, or pearl barley, from which all partook of a morsel, leaving the remains on the graves for the souls of the dead. One of the elders was master of ceremonies. The ritual invocation, as recollected by the informant many years after and promptly committed to paper by Swianiewiczowa, was as follows:

> Elder: W hosci my k' wam pryszli
> Chorus: Dziady, dziady
> Elder: Malaczko pryniasli
> Chorus: Dziady, dziady
> Elder: Kaszu, miodu niasli
> Chorus: Dziady, dziady
> Elder: Nia bojcias duszy,
>   ni ksiandzou, ni papou,
>   sami swai pryszli.
> Chorus: Dziady, dziady
> Elder: Jeszcie, pijcie duszy
> Chorus: Dziady, dziady
> Elder: Jeszcze, pijcie usie
> Chorus: Dziady, dziady.[52]

After her marriage, but before being forced to leave her native region for good in 1919, Lisowska attended *dziady* ceremonies a couple of times in the village of Uhły near her husband's estate of Woronecz, also in the district of Lepel. Although the ceremony was virtually identical with that observed in Bobynicze, the invocation was differently worded; but Lisowska could not remember it in later life.[53]

7

In May 1919 Olimpia Zambrzycka volunteered as a courier in the Polska Organizacja Wojskowa and completed her schooling in Chełmno, Pomerania, in a school catering for children evacuated from Eastern Poland. Following the Treaty of Riga, the new Polish–Russian frontier passed through the grounds of the Wiazyń estate. A frontier

---

[50] 'Interpretacja', 55.

[51] In Swianiewiczowa's letter to Pigoń of 29 Nov. 1965 (n. 20) the village is twice referred to as Babynicze.

[52] Swianiewiczowa, 'Interpretacja', 55; also in letter to Pigoń dated 20 Oct. 1965 (n. 20). In her letter of 29 Nov. 1965 she mentions that Lisowska consistently referred to the Elder as *zapiewajło*.

[53] 'Interpretacja', 56.

watch-tower (*strażnica*) was set up in the manor-house. One hundred hectares of the property became Soviet territory; the 200 hectares remaining on the Polish side were incorporated into the commune of Radoszkowice in the district of Mołodeczno. At the King Stefan Batory University in Wilno Zambrzycka studied first natural sciences, then geography.[54] In 1926 she married Stanisław Swianiewicz, then a lecturer in political economy at the university. From 1928 she taught geography at secondary-school level, retaining her interest in folkloric customs. In a conversation with me in the summer of 1987, her widower recalled how, when all the horses were needed in the fields at harvest-time, she would walk miles across country to talk in secrecy to some witch about her lore and practices, advisedly leaving her husband on the outskirts of the village, well out of earshot.

By the beginning of this century, *dziady* as an outdoor ceremony was all but extinct. The fact that it survived long enough to be observed by Lisowska is explained by Swianiewiczowa in terms of the strength of the Uniate tradition in the Witebsk area, and of the popular cult of St Josaphat, which was undoubtedly boosted by his relatively recent canonization.[55] There were, however, instances in the inter-war period of the ceremony's revival *al fresco*. The field research of the Belorussian literary scholar Stanisław Stankiewicz in the villages of Olchówka and Malewo in the district of Nieśwież convinced him that the autumn *dziady* were celebrated both indoors and at the cemetery.[56] Similarly, when the Orthodox church in the village of Sieniawka (district of Nieśwież) was restored to the Uniates at the request of the local population, the return of the parishioners to the tradition of their forebears resulted in the renewed celebration of *dziady* at the cemetery. Food was brought and left on the tombs. After the priest had prayed and consecrated the graves, old people summoned spirits. On returning from the cemetery, a banquet (*stypa*) was held at home.[57]

8

Swianiewiczowa spent the Second World War first in Wilno, teaching on courses for adults, then, with her children, on the Wiazyń estate,

[54] Her MA dissertation, entitled 'Tarasy Prawilii w dolinie Waki', was published by the Towarzystwo Przyjaciół Nauki in Wilno in 1932.

[55] 'Interpretacja', 45–6. A major propagator of the Uniate Church, Bishop Josaphat of Polotsk, was murdered by the inhabitants of Witebsk in 1623. He was canonized in 1867. See D. H. Farmer, *The Oxford Dictionary of Saints*, 2 ed. (Oxford–New York, 1989), s.v.

[56] Stankiewicz, *Pierwiastki* (n. 49), 177; also quoted in 'Interpretacja', 42.

[57] 'Interpretacja', 42–3. Despite the enforcement of Orthodoxy, the population of Sieniawka had continued to say the Angelus and Hail Mary in Polish. Swianiewiczowa's source (Antoni Bubień from the village of Jefimowicze, as reported to her by Maria Wołodkowicz) had been terrified of the *dziady* ceremony in childhood, and retained memories of awe, mystery, and dread (ibid.).

which had been nationalized following the German invasion and where she worked as a book-keeper. Contact was maintained with Janka Kupala's widow. In July 1944 the Soviet Army occupied Sieledczyki. The NKVD followed shortly after. Wiazyń was converted into the *Kolkhoz imeni Kirova* and subsequently renamed after Janka Kupala.[58] With her father and children Swianiewiczowa moved to the *khutar* of Hurnowicze, once part of the family estate. In 1946 she decided to rejoin her husband in the West; in the event, she was to spend the next ten years as a geography teacher in Tczew, Pomerania. In view of her impending 'repatriation', she was advised against visiting Kupala's widow, whose home in Minsk was then under surveillance, at the same time as the house of the poet's birth was being set up as a museum. Through a mutual friend, however, she learned of the circumstances surrounding the poet's 'accidental' death in Moscow.[59]

Referring later to this period, Olimpia stated that up to the time when she was forced to leave Sieledczyki local belief in the power and presence of ancestral spirits was unabated. Throughout the war the village women continued to believe that spotted sheep were the result of a housewife's having done her darning on a holy evening.[60] Village opinion in Sieledczyki was that the young man denounced for enlisting the help of German soldiers to persuade a farmer into allowing a dance on Whit Monday and subsequently removed to a forced-labour camp by the NKVD, had been punished by the spirits of the dead for failing to observe their cult.[61] At what may have been the last *dziady* ceremony attended by Swianiewiczowa 'the following people were remembered: a young man hanged by the Germans; a Polish teacher from the neighbouring village murdered by Russian partisans; and a lady, the owner of a big estate, who was murdered during the War, leaving two little daughters and an aged mother'.[62]

In 1957, after seventeen years' separation, Swianiewiczowa rejoined her husband in Indonesia. During her year's stay in Jogjakarta in Central Java, living close to the Chinese cemetery, she had ample opportunity to observe Chinese practices connected with the cult of the dead. Night-time ceremonies with chanting and dishes of food left by the tombs were closely reminiscent of the rites in Sieledczyki.[63] A year later in London she renewed contact with Professor Cezaria Ehren-

[58] After the war the manor-house was dismantled and transported to another district (letter from St. Swianiewicz to Nina Taylor dated 5 Nov. 1987).

[59] Janka Kupala died on 28 June 1942 'in mysterious circumstances, falling down the well of the stairs of his Moscow hotel'. See McMillin, *History* (n. 24), 195. According to a manuscript note by Olimpia Swianiewiczowa entitled 'Okruchy wiadomości o Janku Kupale' (PISM, shelf-mark KOL 261), Kupala's widow was convinced that her husband had been murdered and this belief was shared by the peasants of Sieledczyki.

[60] *Sift*, 44.   [61] Ibid. 45.   [62] Ibid. 42.

[63] See O. Swianiewiczowa, 'Dziady chińskie a dziady białoruskie', *Tydzień Polski*, 23 Dec. 1972, p. 4.

kreutz (later Jędrzejewicz, née Baudouin de Courtenay), whose seminars in ethnography she had once attended at the Stefan Batory University in Wilno, and began reading widely on the background of her subject.[64]

At about this time Stanisław Pigoń was working on his second major study of Mickiewicz's *Dziady*[65] and entered into correspondence with Swianiewiczowa, asking numerous detailed questions concerning all aspects of the *dziady* ritual.[66] Their range and detail would seem to suggest his own numerous reservations on the subject. Specifically, he wanted to know if the prototype for Mickiewicz's drama was *radawnica* (as described by Czarnowska) or the autumn *dziady*. In particular, his questions about the denominational associations of the ceremony indicate a somewhat blurred awareness of Orthodox, Uniate, and Roman Catholic relations in the border provinces between Russia and Poland.

In her replies, Swianiewiczowa provided Pigoń with much of the information, already presented in this article, that would subseqently form the backbone of her 'Interpretacja'.[67] She also made it unmistakably clear that *radawnica* and *dziady* were not the same thing. *Dziady*, a traditional folk custom going back to pre-Christian times, was an act of *communion* with the dead, whereas *radawnica*, which had been introduced in her part of Belorussia by the Orthodox Church in the nineteenth century after the abolition of the Uniate Church, was an act of *commemoration* of the dead.

Although most of her evidence amounted to a rebuttal of his line of thought, Pigoń stuck to his guns. Work on his book was at an advanced stage, and it may have been too late for him to change tack. He does, it is true, adduce some of Swianiewiczowa's evidence in his book.[68] Though fully aware that the Uniates in the province of Nowogródek used Polish prayers, he refers to 'the fundamentally Catholic structure (*osnowa*) of the ceremony'.[69] Despite the hints provided by the poet himself, he is adamant in stating that Mickiewicz was present at the springtime *radawnica*,[70] in other words, at the ritual which Czarnowska described in 1817. Pigoń refers to it as 'a relic of Slavonic mythology that she defended against prejudices concerning its religious impropriety'.[71] He intended to treat it as a variant of *dziady* on the grounds that only *radawnica* is a communal experience, held in the cemetery of a Russian Orthodox church, or on the graves, in the presence of a priest,

---

[64] The upshot was two lectures, 'Pogrzeby' (n. 17) and 'Dziady białoruskie' (n. 36). In her first letter to Pigoń (n. 20) she mentions that they were compiled from memory.

[65] St. Pigoń, *Formowanie 'Dziadów', części drugiej: Rekonstrukcja genetyczna* (Warsaw, 1967).

[66] See n. 20. [67] See n. 16.

[68] See Pigoń, *Formowanie* (n. 65), 21. [69] Ibid. 20.

[70] 'upatrywać należy właśnie w wiosennym obrzędzie . . .' (ibid. 13).

[71] Ibid. 34.

and involving not just one family but a group of families, who would feast first alone and then communally. The autumn *dziady*, on the other hand, were celebrated privately, within the family circle at home. On the strength of this analysis, he interprets *radawnica* as a ritual of communion with the dead.[72] He said in a letter to Swianiewiczowa, 'Perhaps it [sc. the interpretation] will not be accurate, but it will be in the style of Mickiewicz, because he too treats it [sc. the ritual] not as a domestic, but as a public ceremony.'[73]

At the same time, Pigoń was aware that the state of research on *dziady* remained unsatisfactory. Writing to Swianiewiczowa after the publication of his book,[74] he admitted to having relied too heavily on sources connected with different territories and rooted in totally different cultural traditions, whose evidence is irrelevant to the study of *Dziady* and misleading. He conceded that he had been unable to break through the divergencies and discrepancies of witnesses.[75] It was in the light of this realization that he deposited her letters in the Jagellonian Library in the hope that they would one day be of use to scholars and stimulate further research.

9

For Swianiewiczowa, the chief interpretative error stems from ignorance of Uniate Church history. Her argument,[76] summarized briefly, is as follows. Whereas the Roman Catholic and Orthodox Churches introduced their own feasts for the dead, the Uniate Church had forborne to intervene in the old pagan ritual of *dziady* or to forbid the bringing and leaving of food on the graves. Inspired by the example of the Jesuit missionaries in China who had ordered their priests to attend Chinese rituals in honour of dead ancestors, an attempt to Christianize the pagan ritual was initiated by a resolution of the Synod of Zamość in 1720. Uniate priests were accordingly encouraged to attend *dziady* celebrations with their parishioners and say the Angelus, Hail Mary, and Eternal Rest, which had been incorporated in the Uniate liturgy by the same Synod. It had also introduced canonical hours, the Rosary and all the litanies, the feast of Corpus Christi, and Latinized liturgical objects such as pulpits, chalices, gonfalons, and confessionals. All these changes became popular among the peasants.

Half a century later the first partition of the Polish–Lithuanian Commonwealth (1772) resulted in the forced conversion of the Uniates

[72] Pigoń, *Formowanie* (n. 65), 21.
[73] See Swianiewiczowa, 'Spór' (n. 20).
[74] Ibid.
[75] Fourth letter of Pigoń to Swianiewiczowa (n. 20).
[76] 'Interpretacja', ch. 2, 'Likwidacja Unii Kościelnej', 32–50.

to Orthodoxy in the territories annexed by Russia. By the time of the second partition in 1793, Uniates in the provinces of Nowogródek and Minsk, being well aware of their probable fate, fled *en masse* to the woods,[77] and became the new social category of 'pilgrims' familiar to Swianiewiczowa from her childhood years.

Although there was some respite in the persecution of Uniates during the reign of Paul I and early years of Alexander I,[78] the gradual elimination of the Uniate Church proceeded steadily. As the chief obstacle to the union of the Orthodox and Uniate Churches was the people's attachment to their priests, ceremonies, shrines, and churches, following the reforms of the Synod of Zamość, the first blow was aimed at these reforms and priests were forbidden to attend *dziady* in the hope that their hold on the faithful would be thereby diminished. Unnoticed at first, this directive was particularly highlighted by the censor's request that the priest and the Roman Catholic prayers be expurgated from the draft text of Mickiewicz's *Dziady*. The fact that it is only Uniates that celebrate *dziady* is fundamental to the interpretation of Mickiewicz's dramatic poem. As the rite was found exclusively among Uniates, its abolition was connected with the abolition of the Union. In attempting to sever the peasantry from its attachment to the Uniate Church the Russian authorities were at the same time trying to destroy other elements of family tradition that pre-dated the Union. Such, according to Swianiewiczowa, was the situation in the villages of Belorussia in Mickiewicz's time. This, then, was the context in which the celebration of *dziady* was driven from the cemetery to the cottage, and which Pigoń and other scholars had failed to understand. For over a century 'the peasant huts and village tombs played the same role in preserving the tradition of the Church Union as the catacombs had played in the early centuries of Christianity'.[79] These aspirations of the Belorussian peasantry to maintain its cultural identity are echoed in Mickiewicz's *Dziady*.

Severer repressions came into force after the official abolition of the Uniate Church in 1839 in the aftermath of the unsuccessful November Rising of 1830.[80] The village of Sieledczyki somehow escaped this fate until the intense Russification programme enforced after the rising of

---

[77] Disguised reference to this is to be found in Ewa Felińska, *Pamiętniki z życia* [. . .], i (Wilno 1856), 31–2. Quoted in 'Interpretacja', 58.

[78] 'Interpretacja', 34–5. The same period appears in a more favourable light in James T. Flynn, 'Josaphat Bułhak: The Last Metropolitan of the Uniate Church in the Russian Empire. A Case Study in the History of Churches in Byelorussia', a paper delivered at the conference 'Christianity and the Byelorussian People', held on 1–2 Oct. 1988 at the Francis Skaryna Byelorussian Library in London. Publication forthcoming.

[79] 'Interpretacja', 26.

[80] Bishop Józef Siemaszko's plan for the abolition of the Uniate Church in fact preceded the Rising by a few years. See E. Likowski, *Dzieje Kościoła Unickiego na Litwie i Rusi w XVIII i XIX wieku uważane głównie ze względu na przyczyny jego upadku* [. . .], 2 ed. (Warsaw, 1906), pt. 2, p. 43.

1863. Swianiewiczowa grew up in awareness of the forced conversion of the Belorussians to Orthodoxy. From childhood conversations with the Sieledczyki swineherd Bazyli Szarenda, with older villagers such as Iljuk Szarenda, and with Łukasz Hryszel from the village of Krynice, she knew how the local Uniate church 'on the tombs' (*na grobach*), built by her great-grandfather, had been converted by force in 1865. The parishioners defending their church had been routed by Cossacks with whips.[81]

To overcome the problem of local attachment to religious practices, the Russian authorities gradually implanted a new tradition, namely *radawnica*,[82] a feast commemorating the dead held on the Tuesday after Low Sunday. The vernal *radawnica* was thus imposed by the Russian clergy after the abolition of the Uniate Church as a substitute for the autumnal *dziady*. It was intended to wean the Belorussian peasantry away from Uniate allegiance and was alien to Belorussian tradition. It is demonstrated in the scene described by Czarnowska, and also in Lednicki's memoirs and elsewhere.[83]

Once *radawnica* had been imposed, the peasants availed themselves of the opportunity to postpone or bring forward their family celebration of *przykładziny*,[84] the ceremony that marked the end of the first year of mourning and at which a new cross was consecrated to replace the one provisionally erected at the funeral. By combining *przykładziny* with *radawnica* the peasants in effect received their mass free of charge.[85] After the consecration, the women spread a cloth on the grave and laid out some vodka and light snacks for the helpers.[86]

The new festival was not a total success with the Belorussian peasantry. Swianiewiczowa concludes[87] that *radawnica* was celebrated in the districts of Czerykow (province of Mohylew), Mozyr (province of Minsk), and in Polesie—and none of these regions is adjacent to

---

[81] 'Interpretacja', 5.

[82] Swianiewiczowa suggests it was launched initially in the Ukraine, where there was a similar spring festival known as *krasna hirka*. In fact, the celebration of *radawnica* ('a feast at which the dead rejoice') at the beginning of St Thomas's Week in areas of Russia and the Ukraine is noted as early as 1372 in the *Troitskaya letopsis'*. See O. Voropay, *Zvychayi nashoho narodu: Etnohrafichnyi narys*, pt. 2 (1966), 9–20, where there is also an account of *krasna hirka* ('the feast of *krasna wiosna*, at which supernatural creatures disport themselves in the valleys and hills'), ibid. 21–6.

[83] W. Lednicki, *Pamiętniki*, i (London, 1963), 252.

[84] 'Interpretacja', 37–9.

[85] This gave rise to a proverb: 'Iszou pop kala kop, a kapa kola papa, a czyrwonyje istużki kala kapieluszki' ('The [Orthodox] priest walked past the hayricks, the hayrick past the priest, and the red ribbons slipped past the [priest's] hat'). Swianiewiczowa explains that the hayricks symbolize the mourners by the graves (ibid. 37–8).

[86] As Swianiewiczowa points out (ibid.), this would appear to be confirmed by Count E. Tyszkiewicz in *Rzut oka na źródła archeologii krajowej, czyli opisanie zabytków niektórych staro-żytności, odkrytych w zachodnich guberniach Cesarstwa Rosyjskiego* [. . .] (Wilno, 1842), 4. In his account of customs in 'Litwa południowa', in the vicinity of the Berezyna, *radawnica* is described as a memorial mass and individual feast held one year after someone's death.

[87] 'Interpretacja', 44–7.

Mickiewicz's native province of Nowogródek. It was not, however, known in the districts of Słonin, Wołkowysk and Minsk, where the number of Basilian monasteries is indicative of Uniate and Roman Catholic preponderance, nor in the provinces of Grodno and Witebsk, where the Uniate rite had taken deep roots following the martyrdom of St Josaphat.

Far from eradicating all customs dating back to Uniate times, forcibly imposed Orthodoxy deepened the people's attachment to those customs. The Belorussian peasant 'at every opportunity, in every conversation, turned his thoughts to the question of that forcible conversion and the problem of returning to the faith of his fathers'.[88] In the village of Sieledczyki, *radawnica* encountered hostile opposition from the peasants. Swianiewiczowa, who had had ample opportunity to participate in local activities and to observe events at the cemetery from the windows of the Wiazyń manor-house, heard about *radawnica* for the first time at an ethnography seminar held in Wilno by Professor Ehrenkreutz. When she later asked a local woman, she was told that 'Radaunica heto pominki, a nie Dziady' ('*Radawnica* is a funeral banquet, not *dziady*').[89]

In other words, *dziady* were celebrated in actual communion with the dead, unlike *radawnica*, which merely commemorated them. This point, as Swianiewiczowa mentions in a letter to Pigoń, was confirmed by Lisowska. The Sieledczyki villagers added, moreover, that 'Radounicu uwiou pop Żelazouskij, a pierad tym nichto ab nijakaj radounicy nia wiedau' ('*Radawnica* was introduced by the Orthodox priest Żelazawski; before that no one knew of any *radawnica*').[90] This was further corroborated by a letter Swianiewiczowa received from her sister, who remembered once hearing the following saying in childhood: 'In Radoszkowicze Mrs Śnitko and Żelazawski introduced *radawnica*, for previously this custom did not exist.'[91] A crossed-out jotting in Swianiewiczowa's notebook mentions the indignant reply of her informant to the effect that 'dziady przychodziac wieczarom jak sciamnieja a nikoli u dzien' ('*dziady* comes at evening when it is getting dark and never in the day').[92] Olimpia herself could remember 'absolutely nothing else' about *radawnica*.[93]

[88] Swianiewiczowa, 'Pogrzeby' (n. 17), 82–3; also 'Interpretacja', 1.
[89] Swianiewiczowa, 'Dziady białoruskie' (n. 36), 90; also quoted by Pigoń, *Formowanie* (n. 65), 21.
[90] 'Interpretacja', 37.
[91] For their services in quelling the Rising of 1863 the Śnitko family received the estate of Karlsberg (or Karlinsberg, formerly Huje, situated some 5 km. as the crow flies from the village of Sieledczyki), which had been confiscated from the Wołodkowicz family for supporting the Rising. See Swianiewiczowa, 'Pamiętnik' (n. 28).
[92] Ibid.
[93] Swianiewiczowa's letter to Pigoń of 29 Nov. 1965 (n. 20).

10

This article has by no means exhausted the topic of Swianiewiczowa's dispute with the accepted body of *Dziady* criticism, and her reservations are not restricted to Pigoń's work alone. Basically, her own experience inclines her to confirm the validity of sources dismissed by other Mickiewicz scholars.[94] As for the oft-invoked Czarnowska, she drily comments on the alacrity with which that lady felt inspired by Count Razumovsky's *Instructions* published in the *Dziennik Wileński* to encourage study of the rural population's customs and superstitions and proceeded to describe a 'tradition' freshly imposed by the Orthodox Church.[95] In the light of the foregoing, one cannot help noting the irony whereby Pigoń, proposing a solution that he hoped would be 'in the spirit of Mickiewicz', produced in effect an argument that is the very antithesis of the Philomath policy and world-view. While the local Belorussian peasants resisted the imposition of *radawnica*, a page of nineteenth-century history was effectively kept blank until the second half of the twentieth through the ingenuous, though unwitting, connivance of Mickiewicz specialists, whose ignorance of regional history amounts to accepting Russification as a *fait accompli*.

Swianiewiczowa's study of the ethnographic and folkloric background of *Dziady* enabled her, moreover, to identify its entire dramatic structure as a projection of the Belorussian annual cycle of ancestor celebration,[96] heralded by the Prologue, in which the date 1 November (falling within the period of the autumn *dziady*) is unambiguously inscribed on the wall by Konrad, and concluded by the Epilogue (Scene 9), which also occurs on Forefathers' Eve. Though predominantly viewed as a patriotic, political, and Messianistic drama, *Dziady* (Part 3) also fits into this scheme, as its scenic sequence takes us through the main holy days devoted to communion with the dead.

If *Dziady* (Part 3) is viewed as a tripartite structure, the central part of the triptych (Father Piotr's vision in Scene 5) takes place at the time of the Easter *dziady*, identified by Swianiewiczowa as children's *dziady*, hence the relevance of his vision of Polish youth being deported to the north. It is flanked by two side-panels. The first consists of Scenes 1 to 4 (the suffering nation), which take place during the winter *dziady* at the winter solstice in the innocent expectation of Christ's birth. Scenes 6 to 8 in the second panel (Muscovite overlords and their Polish henchmen)

[94] For instance, she defends the evidence supplied by Tyszkiewicz (*Rzut oka* (n. 86)) against Wantowska's suggestion ('*Dziady*' (n. 15), 232) that he based his knowledge of *dziady* practices on Mickiewicz's poem rather than on first-hand acquaintance with the ritual ('Interpretacja', 52).
[95] 'Interpretacja', 92–4.
[96] Ibid. 103–54.

take place around St John's Eve, at the time of the summer solstice. Within this framework, each of the three *dziady* cycles—Christmas, Easter, and St John's Eve—provides one scene for Part 3's small central triptych of dreams (Ewa, Father Piotr, and Nowosilcow). The Warsaw drawing-room (Scene 7) alone falls outside this pattern: it lies beyond the cultural orbit of Belorussian practices and beliefs, and is therefore not affected by the other world. While *Dziady* realizes the ideal of Romantic aesthetics whereby each work has its own composition, the reality, spirituality, and structure of the play as a whole are rooted in the pagan–Christian ritual calendar of the Belorussian Uniate village.

11

Writing shortly before her death in 1974,[97] faced with the difficulty of establishing what is real in Mickiewicz's *Dziady*, and what belongs to pure fantasy, Swianiewiczowa considered her research to be in no way conclusive: she felt that the debate had not yet been fully resolved, that the question of the prototype was still unanswered, and that she had at best highlighted the problem. Among other points, she was unable to explain how the four villages in the vicinity of the Zambrzycki estate survived the abolition of the Uniate Church in 1839, and were only 'converted' to Orthodoxy in 1865. She further considered that Russian policy in the partitioned territories of the erstwhile Grand Duchy of Lithuania and the ban on giving a Christian character to the ancient *dziady* ceremony was a question awaiting not only the ethnographer, but also the political historian. She thus saw her own contribution less as an answer than as a challenge for future scholars.

The evidence she adduces and her own line of argument do, however, confirm that Mickiewicz's *Dziady* is neither literary fiction nor 'documentary ethnography',[98] but a case of folkloristic realism, based on the liturgical calendar and underpinned by the system of deeper belief characteristic of the Belorussian peasantry. It shows furthermore that: 'The Belorussian village, in other words the descendants of the Krivichians and the Dregovichians, had preserved the purest Slavonic traditions and many elements of spiritual culture that had vanished elsewhere, but were once common to the peoples of Asia and Europe alike.'[99] Her experience and reflections bear out almost to the letter the comments of a nineteenth-century witness, writing about the village of Komarowicze in the district of Mozyr, to the effect that the Belorussian imagination 'was able to hear, see, smell, and touch supernatural and

[97] Swianiewiczowa, 'Spór' (n. 20).
[98] 'Interpretacja', 4–6. The term is used by Wantowska, '*Dziady*' (n. 15), 290.
[99] Swianiewiczowa, 'Dziady chińskie' (n. 63), 4.

purely spiritual phenomena: within their imaginative world, the dead walked about no less normally than the living'.[100] Pigoń referred to Swianiewiczowa as the last eye-witness of the *dziady* ritual. Her own uncertainties notwithstanding, her intimate knowledge of local territory and peasant spirituality alike provide a more satisfactory starting-point than other material published to date.

---

[100] E[mma] Jeleńska, 'Wieś Komarowicze w pow. Mozyrskim', *Wisła*, v (1891), 290–331 and 480–520. Quoted in 'Interpretacja', 44 and 3.

Dal''s *Dictionary* and the Censorship: New Material on Baudouin de Courtenay

By A. V. BLYUM

THE years 1903–9 saw the achievement of a major publishing undertaking: the third edition of V. I. Dal''s celebrated *Tolkovyi slovar' zhivogo velikorusskogo yazyka*.[1] The editor of this new edition was Ivan Aleksandrovich (Jan Niecisław) Baudouin de Courtenay, at that time a professor of St Petersburg University. Baudouin's keen social sense and independence of mind, his outright and determined rejection of autocracy in all its manifestations—especially where it impinged on scholarship and culture—brought him into strained relations with the bureaucracy of the Ministry of Education, the censorship, and other custodial institutions of the tsarist state. Relations became particularly strained in the course of his work as editor of Dal''s *Dictionary*. Recently discovered censorship documents make it possible to present a clear picture of the reaction of the authorities to this edition.

It is known that, when preparing the new edition of the *Dictionary*, Baudouin approached his task with the utmost reverence for this outstanding monument of Russian lexicography and determined to preserve it in its original form. At the same time, without distorting the fabric of the *Dictionary*, he wished to supplement it with new material that had appeared in recent years. He extracted an abundance of such material from contemporary journals, left-wing newspapers, and court reports. As well as material from these sources, he included in his 'supplements to Dal'' items which he had personally collected over many years in different parts of Russia. New words and phraseology which he introduced were set off from Dal''s text in square brackets. By the inclusion of this material Dal''s *Dictionary* was in no way 'spoilt'—it was, on the contrary, enriched.

The publication of the first volume of the new edition (1903) and, more particularly, the second and third volumes (1905, 1907) created a

[1] The first edition of Dal''s *Dictionary* was published in 1863–6 and was followed by a second, revised and expanded, edition in 1880–2. Baudouin's edition of 1903–9 (the third) was reprinted in 1912. There have been subsequent reprintings of the second edition in Moscow and of the third edition in Paris. For previous studies of Baudouin's edition, see Joachim Mugdan, *Jan Baudouin de Courtenay (1845–1929): Leben und Werk* (Munich, 1984), 91–2.

veritable storm in the press. The reactionary press attacked the new edition on the 'academic' grounds that 'Baudouin had "spoiled" Dal''. In reality, the conservative journalists (especially those of Suvorin's *Novoe vremya*) were much disconcerted by the additional items which Baudouin had drawn from the phraseology current in the turbulent years leading up to the 1905 Revolution. In an article 'Newspaper Hounding of the Third Edition of Dal's *Dictionary*' Baudouin tartly ridiculed the strained critical efforts of the conservatives and explained the purpose and nature of the supplementary material he had introduced.[2]

What position did the organs of officialdom adopt in this polemic? From the documents cited below it is clear that from the outset they gave firm support to the journalists of the extreme right, employing their own particular methods for 'conducting polemical debate'. In the first place, certain 'volunteer' censors came forward to alert the Directorate of Censorship to the highly 'inflammatory' nature of Baudouin's additions (the *Dictionary* was subject only to corrective, not preliminary, censorship). One of the first to take on the function of unofficial censor was the Governor of Chernigov, who in December 1904 sent to N. A. Zverev, the then head of the Directorate of Censorship, the following indignant letter:

Dear Sir,

A third edition of Dal''s *Tolkovyi slovar' zhivogo velikorusskogo yazyka* is currently being printed by the Wolf Company under the editorship of Professor Baudouin de Courtenay, and in the twelfth issue just published on p. 337 under the word *kokarda* ['cockade'] a definition is given of the word *kokardnik* ['cockade-wearer']; the latter word does not appear at all in the 1881 edition of the dictionary, and the new edition, in attempting to gloss it, not only defines it incorrectly, but supports the definition it gives by an example which is nonsensical in essence and extremely inflammatory in purpose.[3]

The Governor enclosed with his letter a copy of the twelfth issue in which the offending place was thickly marked with green pencil. Here Baudouin had provided an example of the use of *kokardnik* which reflected the deep hostility felt by the democratic elements of society for the higher echelons of officialdom: '«Кокардник», «краснополкладочник» — значит «прохвост»'.[4] The Governor ended his letter:

If I could light by chance on one such trick [perpetrated] by the publishers or editor, you can well imagine how many glosses of a similar kind may be found in this corrected

---

[2] *Izvestiya Knizhnogo magazina Tovarishchestva M. O. Vol'f*, 1907 no. 1, p. 5.

[3] Tsentral'nyi gosudarstvennyi istoricheskii arkhiv (TsGIA), Leningrad, *fond* 777, *opis'* 5, 1904, *delo* 211, *list* 1.

[4] '"Cockade-wearer", "red-lining-wearer"—that means "blackguard"'; the references are to the cap insignia and tunic-linings of senior officials.

and supplemented version of the serious academic work which Dal''s *Dictionary* is. I regard it as my duty to report this matter for Your Excellency's consideration.

The censorship authority in St Petersburg 'noted' this denunciation by the Chernigov 'philologist', but any intended repressive measures against the *Dictionary* were forestalled by the events of 1905 and the consequent reform of censorship control which made the matter one of secondary concern.

A more clearly defined and unambiguous approach to the new edition of the *Dictionary* was taken by the so-called 'pedagogic' censorship, for which the Special Section of the Advisory Committee (*Uchenyi komitet*) of the Ministry of Education was responsible. This Section had been established in 1869 for the specific purpose of preventing the percolation of 'undesirable' literature into the libraries of schools and free public reading-rooms and had the dismal distinction of having banned many outstanding works of literature (it had to its credit the withdrawal from library circulation of works by Pushkin, Lermontov, Nekrasov, Saltykov-Shchedrin, and other classic authors). In 1906, vol. 3 of Baudouin's edition of Dal''s *Dictionary* came to the Advisory Committee to be approved for use in libraries. I. A. Shlyapkin, a member of the Committee, reported on this volume to the Minister of Education as follows:

The decision to recommend the *Dictionary* was based on the inspection of the first issue (1903). The Advisory Committee, trusting in the acknowledged scholarly standing of Professor Baudouin de Courtenay, departed in that case from its usual practice and did not await the appearance of all [further] issues of the edition, fairly assuming that the Professor's name was sufficient guarantee of the soundness of any amendments and additions which might be introduced into the *Dictionary* and of the scrupulousness of the editing. The present issue, however, convinces [us] that the *Dictionary* is not being prepared in exactly the way the Committee would have expected. Examples included in the present issue are wholly inappropriate. In the circumstances there can naturally be no question of the recommendation remaining in force.[5]

The Advisory Committee fully agreed with Shlyapkin's view and made the following resolution: 'In view of the inappropriateness of the phraseological examples, the Advisory Committee resolves that this publication in all its parts should be excluded from the books recommended for the libraries of schools and free public libraries and reading-rooms.'[6]

What exactly were the phraseological examples that the Advisory Committee deemed 'inappropriate'? In his report Shlyapkin noted: 'A strange impression, to say the least, is created by the commentaries on

[5] TsGIA, *fond* 734, *opis'* 3, 1906, *delo* 113, *list* 680.
[6] Ibid., *list* 682.

the words *parazit* and *patriot*.'[7] The examples to illustrate these words had been taken by Baudouin from publicistic works that were progressive, if not actually social-democratic, in character. For instance, the sample use given for *parazit* reads:

Черная сотня—явление, несомненно, *паразитарное*, и потому мы вправе ожидать в нем атрофию многих человеческих признаков и, взамен, усиленное развитие других. Невозможно перечислить все те случаи, когда в народной жизни, в жизни и русского общества выступают на сцену эти паразиты...[8]

Similarly characteristic and expressive is the example provided for the word *patriot*:

Непризванные носители истинно-русских идеалов, все эти Крушеваны и Карлы-Амалии Грингмуты,[9] находят возможным выступать в качестве выразителей истинно-русских стремлений, истинно-русских патриотов и призывать к избиению изменников... Патриотизм охранников-хулиганов и «черной сотни» прямо пропорционален возможности безнаказанно грабить... *Потреотизм* связан непременно с невежеством и запросами зверских инстинктов: «раззудись плечо—размахнись рука». На знамени черной сотни пишется символ веры «рррусского потреотизма».[10]

The choice of these particular examples indicates that Baudouin had set out to express in original form—by the use of illustrative phraseology—his ironic and sharply negative attitude to the ignorant clique which led the Black Hundred Union of St Michael the Archangel. And it is noteworthy that somewhat later, in 1913, the Union took occasion to mount a vicious attack on the new edition of Dal''s *Dictionary*. In a speech to the Duma the head of the Union, V. M. Purishkevich, declared with reference to the Academy of Sciences:

It was revered thirty years ago, but since politics has gained a footing in the Academy, when even on such classic works of Russian Slavonic scholarship as that of Dal'

[7] TsGIA, *fond* 733, *opis'* 196, *delo* 144, *list* 363.
[8] 'The Black Hundred is indubitably a *parasitic* phenomenon and we may therefore expect to find in it the atrophying of many human qualities and the corresponding development of others. It is impossible to enumerate all the occasions on which these parasites manifest themselves in the life of the people and, indeed, also in the life of Russian society . . .'.
[9] Leaders of the Black Hundred Union of St Michael the Archangel.
[10] 'The self-appointed bearers of true Russian ideals, all those Krushevans and Karl Amaliya Gringmuths who find it possible to present themselves as the spokesmen of true Russian aspirations, as the true Russian patriots, and to call for the slaughter of all traitors . . . The patriotism of reactionary hooligans and of the "Black Hundred" is directly proportionate to the scope [afforded them] to pillage with impunity . . . Patriotism is invariably linked with ignorance and the demands of brute instincts: "If your shoulder gets the feeling, let your arm take a swing." The creed of Russian patriotism is inscribed on the banner of the Black Hundred.' The illiterate form of the word *patriotizm* (*potreotizm*) may be related to a passage in Saltykov-Shchedrin's *Sovremennaya idilliya*. The account given there of the First Guild merchant Paramonov, which consists solely of a tariff-list of all that he has expended in the course of his life, includes the item: 'In 1877 to the precinct [police] to show patriotism (*na potreotizm*)—95,000 roubles' (M. E. Saltykov-Shchedrin, *Sobranie sochinenii* (M., 1965–77), xv(1), 198).

Academician Baudouin de Courtenay[11] permits himself to perform an operation by scalp[ing] (*putem skalpa*), it is difficult to speak of the impartiality of the Academy of Sciences, [and] difficult to speak of its scholarly merits.[12]

Undoubtedly, the reason for this malicious attack is largely to be explained by the substance of the phraseological examples included in the new edition of the *Dictionary* which were cited above. Characteristically, the Advisory Committee, despite its continual claims to be 'impartial' and 'above party interest', proved in its assessment of the *Dictionary* to be entirely at one with the most rabid representatives of the Black Hundred.

So the new edition of Dal''s *Dictionary* was excluded from the libraries: by order of a special circular of the Department of the Ministry of Education all the volumes published were removed from the libraries of schools, free libraries, and reading-rooms. The prime explanation of the Advisory Committee's decision was, of course, that this custodial organ of the establishment acted in defence of the extreme reactionary party. The true background for their decision may be more readily understood, though, if a comparison is made between the document of 1906 and another of the previous year. We find that in June 1905 the chairman of the Advisory Committee had approached Baudouin with a request for his opinion on whether three books in Lithuanian might be allowed in libraries in the Baltic territories— 'there being among the members of the Committee no specialists in Lithuanian'. Baudouin gave a high rating to the books in question, but ended his reply by declaring with characteristic forthrightness that 'the Advisory Committee should lay aside its censorship functions' and 'abandon its censor's concern for the intellectual and cultural needs of the populace'.[13] At a special meeting of the Committee the second part of Baudouin's reply was deemed 'inappropriate' (this ritual word was evidently reckoned by members of the Committee to have universal application), since

the functions referred to had never in any true sense of the word come within the sphere of action of the Committee, the Special Section of which was concerned with the scrutiny of books for readers of the common class solely from the point of 'pedagogic censorship', having in view the permissibility of books intended for use in schools and reading-rooms.[14]

Here, the members of the Committee evidently 'forgot' the fact that their 'pedagogic' censorship was more stringent in fact than the general

[11] Baudouin de Courtenay had been a corresponding member of the Academy since 1897, but the Academy itself was not directly concerned with his edition of Dal''s *Dictionary*.
[12] *Stenograficheskii otchet Gosudarstvennoi Dumy, 4-yi sozyv, 1-aya sessiya* (Spb., 1913), 913.
[13] TsGIA, *fond* 734, *opis'* 3, 1905, *delo* 218, *list* 174.
[14] Ibid., *list* 176.

censorship operated by the Ministry of the Interior, and often forbade books which the latter had allowed.

These remarks of Baudouin in his reply sum up the man—his independence, his hatred for all forms of abject loyal zeal; he thought it shameful for anyone associated with the high calling of scholarship to involve himself in the censoring activities of the establishment. It was quite natural that when, a year later, the fate of his edition of Dal''s *Dictionary* depended on their decision, the officials of the Advisory Committee took their opportunity and prohibited its use in libraries. The irony was that by this decision they fully confirmed the recalcitrant scholar's assessment of the Committee's activity which they had vainly striven to disclaim.

The episode of Dal''s *Dictionary* was not the only occasion when Baudouin crossed with the censorship authorities. A few years later, in 1912, the censors insisted on the deletion of a page from Baudouin's short book *Pol'skii yazyk sravnitel'no s russkim i drevne-tserkovno-slavyanskim* (Spb., 1912) because one of the texts for translation contained an exposition of the author's 'radical' views. A sharper brush with the censorship occurred the year after, when the authorities confiscated Baudouin's *Natsional'nyi i territorial'nyi priznak v avtonomii* (Spb., 1913), in which he fiercely denounced the exploitative policy conducted by Russia in relation to its borderlands. Baudouin was tried and sentenced to prison: for several months the distinguished philologist was confined in a political prison—the ill-famed Kresty in St Petersburg.[15]

Such is the history of Baudouin's relations with the censorship institutions of tsarist Russia. The archival documents cited indicate the extremely guarded attitude of these institutions to a branch of learning as 'academic' and 'remote from politics' as philology might at first appear to be. At the same time, these documents throw some added light on the difficult conditions in which Baudouin de Courtenay, one of the leading linguistic scholars of his time, pursued his academic life and, in particular, prepared his edition of the *Dictionary* of V. I. Dal'.

---

[15] On Baudouin's imprisonment, see Mugdan, *Jan Baudouin de Courtenay* (n. 1), 36–8, and A. A. Leont'ev, 'Tvorcheskii put' i osnovnye cherty lingvisticheskoi kontseptsii I. A. Boduena de Kurtene', in: *I. A. Boduen de Kurtene (k 30-letiyu so dnya smerti)* (M., 1960), 24–5.

Mikhail Bulgakov and Lev Tolstoy

By J. LURIA (YA. S. LUR'E)

IN the ever growing and almost too vast literature on Mikhail Bulgakov, the theme of 'Bulgakov and . . .', is one of the most popular. The validity of formulating such a theme is not in doubt; the understanding of any subject may be illuminated by means of comparative analysis. However, the nature of such comparisons may differ and various aims may be pursued. They may be concerned with studying the direct influence of one writer on another, their stylistic manner, or, finally, similarities and differences in their views on the world.

The only study we have of the reflection of Tolstoy's *Voina i mir* in the works of Bulgakov, Volker Levin's article,[1] lacks a clearly defined theme. First of all, Levin examines the influence of other great Russian writers—Pushkin and Dostoevsky—on Bulgakov. Moving then to Tolstoy, the author pays attention to Bulgakov's interesting speech about Tolstoy given at 'Herzen House' in the second half of the 1920s, as recorded by E. Mindlin. He then examines reminiscences of Tolstoy in *Belaya gvardiya* and, in more detail, dwells on Bulgakov's 1931–2 stage adaptation of *Voina i mir*. The article concludes with reference to two other of Bulgakov's adaptations for the stage—*Mertvye dushi* and *Don Kikhot*. However, the significance of Tolstoy's work for Bulgakov the writer remains unexamined in Levin's article.

In E. Mindlin's recollections, although the text can hardly be regarded as an exact reproduction of Bulgakov's words, the most important thing is Bulgakov's statement that 'after Tolstoy it is impossible to live and work in literature as if there had never been any Tolstoy. The fact that he existed—I am not afraid to say, that there existed the phenomenon of Lev Nikolaevich Tolstoy—obliges every Russian writer after Tolstoy . . . to be mercilessly harsh towards himself.'[2]

Tolstoy's influence on Bulgakov is most clearly revealed in *Belaya gvardiya*. To a certain extent this influence was proclaimed even at the time of the novel's composition in 1923. 'After the heavenly thunder (for even heaven's patience has a limit) has killed all contemporary

An Ilchester Lecture given in the Taylor Institution on 18 October 1988.

[1] V. Levin, 'Michail Bulgakov und Lev Tolstoj: Ein Beitrag zur Rezeptionsgeschichte von "Krieg und Freiden"', *Die Welt der Slaven*, xxv (NF iv) (1980), 317–37.

[2] E. Mindlin, *Neobyknovennye sobesedniki: Literaturnye vospominaniya*, 2 ed. (M., 1979), 171; E. S. Bulgakova and S. A. Lyandres (eds.), *Vospominaniya o Mikhaile Bulgakove* (M., 1988), 155–6.

writers to a man and in fifty years' time a new Lev Tolstoy appears, an amazing book about the great battles in Kiev will be created', wrote Bulgakov in the sketch *Kiev-gorod*.[3] Of course, Bulgakov would scarcely have presumed to name his own work, then in process of creation, as this 'amazing book' (his own great book—*Master i Margarita*—he was to write some years later, and its action takes place not in Kiev, but in Moscow and Jerusalem), but his *Belaya gvardiya* was indeed dedicated to 'the great battles in Kiev'.

The similarity between particular images and motifs in *Belaya gvardiya* and *Voina i mir* has more than once been noted. A. Lezhnev, the very first reviewer of the novel when it was published (though not in its entirety, as publication was interrupted) in the journal *Rossiya*, pointed out the similarity. Lezhnev wrote that 'in his treatment of the characters the author tries to follow Lev Tolstoy' and that 'there are also similarities between individual characters of *Belaya gvardiya* and those of Tolstoy; thus, Nikolka Turbin reminds one of Petya Rostov'. Tal'berg's similarity to Tolstoy's Berg has been noted, and so on.[4] Finally, Bulgakov himself in his famous letter to the Soviet Government of 28 March 1930 wrote that the fate of a 'family of the gentry-intelligentsia, cast in the years of the Civil War by an ineluctable fate into the camp of the White guard', had been depicted by him in *Belaya gvardiya* (as, too, in *Dni Turbinykh*) 'in the traditions of *Voina i mir*'.[5]

Tolstoyan motifs are characteristic not only of *Belaya gvardiya*. They can also be noted in *Master i Margarita*. In the critical literature it has already been pointed out that 'like Tolstoi, whose rewriting of the four Gospels has certain things in common with Bulgakov's, the author of the Pilate chapters does not deny the importance of the religious impulse in man', and that 'for both writers, the teachings of the Jesus of the Sermon on the Mount were crucial'.[6] And the words of Ieshua Ha-Notsri which doom him to perish—'All power is violence against people and . . . there will come a time, when there will be neither the power of the Caesars, nor any other power'—represent, of course, the Tolstoyan understanding of Christianity.[7]

But to what extent did Tolstoy's views influence Bulgakov's *Welt-anschauung* as a whole? Regrettably, the link between Bulgakov's philosophy of history and that of Tolstoy has passed unnoticed. In his article on Bulgakov and Tolstoy, Volker Levin, referring to *Belaya*

[3] M. Bulgakov, *Chasha zhizni* (M., 1988), 432.

[4] A. Lezhnev, 'Literaturnye zametki', *Krasnaya nov'*, 1925 kn. 7, pp. 269–70. Cf. M. O. Chudakova, *Mikhail Bulgakov: Pamyatnye literaturnye daty 1981 g.* (M., 1981), 185; L. Yanovskaya, *Tvorcheskii put' Mikhaila Bulgakova* (M., 1983), 8, 133.

[5] *Novyi Mir*, 1987 no. 8, p. 196.

[6] E. Proffer, *Bulgakov: Life and Work* (Ann Arbor, 1984), 541 n. 21.

[7] M. Bulgakov, *Belaya gvardiya. Teatral'nyi roman. Master i Margarita* (M., 1975), 447 (henceforth referred to in the text by the letter B and page number).

gvardiya, wrote that in this novel 'unfortunately, Tolstoy's philosophical-historical reflections are absent'. Nor did Levin find any reflection of Tolstoy's philosophy of history in Bulgakov's stage adaptation of *Voina i mir*, to which his article is largely devoted. Here, according to him, 'the philosophical-historical reflections of the original, which cannot be conveyed by dramatic means, are totally absent'; and 'the philosophical-historical content of the original has not been conveyed'.[8]

In order to assess the validity of these claims, we must turn to the question of Tolstoy's philosophy of history, which has in recent years been examined no less widely than the art of Bulgakov.[9] The fate of Tolstoy's theory of history as set out in *Voina i mir* has not been a very happy one. The philosophical-historical chapters of the novel were repudiated by Turgenev and Flaubert; and other critics did not approve of them either, even those who, like N. Strakhov and N. Akhsharumov, gave a warm welcome to the book as a whole. In recent literature on Tolstoy his philosophical-historical views have likewise failed to receive general recognition.

Isaiah Berlin's essay 'The Hedgehog and the Fox'[10] may be considered to be the most authoritative Western examination of Tolstoy's philosophy of history. Berlin noted that for Tolstoy, as for other Russian writers of the nineteenth century, it was natural to strive to give 'direct answers' to the 'accursed questions' of human and historical existence. In this regard Berlin compares Tolstoy to Marx and, also, to Darwin. 'Like Marx (of whom at the time of writing of *War and Peace* he apparently knew nothing) Tolstoy saw clearly that if history was a science, it must be possible to discover and formulate a set of true laws of history', which would give the possibility of 'predicting' the historical future. These thoughts, it would have seemed, should have led the author to a serious analysis of Tolstoy's 'historical doctrines'. But we find no such an analysis in Berlin's essay. He confined himself to stating that the 'terrible dilemma' between the conformity to laws of the historical process and the free will of separate individuals remained unresolved by Tolstoy.

F. F. Seeley has firmly rejected Tolstoy's views on history. Treating ironically the 'formidable analytical powers' ascribed to Tolstoy, Seeley announces that the writer's deliberations about the role of power in historical events is based on an elementary error in logic. Tolstoy, in Seeley's view, confuses the concept of cause as 'sufficient condition' with the concept of cause as 'necessary condition': in reality, according to Seeley, the power and will of a ruler are not a sufficient condition for

[8] Levin, op. cit. (n. 1), 319, 333.

[9] For a more detailed exposition of this problem, see the articles of Ya. S. Lur'e: (i) 'Differentsial istorii v "Voine i mire"', *Russkaya literatura*, 1978 no. 3, pp. 43–60; (ii) 'Ob istoricheskoi kontseptsii L'va Tolstogo', ibid. 1989 no. 1, pp. 26–43.

[10] I. Berlin, 'The Hedgehog and the Fox', in: idem, *Russian Thinkers* (London, 1978), 22–50.

a historical event to occur, for, in order for this event to occur, an entire complex of other favourable circumstances is needed; but this does not prevent them from being 'necessary conditions'.[11] However, Tolstoy did not take the position Seeley attributes to him. On the contrary, he considered power a necessary condition and, indeed, the only force 'that compels people to direct their activity towards a single goal'. It is precisely this view that expresses his main disagreement with Buckle, an author with whom he was at one in recognizing the existence of laws governing the historical process. For Tolstoy, the concept of power 'is the single handle by means of which it is possible to control the material of history in its present exposition, and he who would break off this handle, as Buckle did, without discovering another method of dealing with historical material, would simply deprive himself of the single available possibility of dealing with it'.[12] But is the power and will of a definite, concrete person a 'necessary condition' of an historical event, and does that person's power serve as proof that precisely that person was pre-ordained to carry out the given historical action? Why does a historical figure in one case achieve success and in another meet with failure? Why in some cases do wars, revolutions, the movement of masses take place, and in other cases fail to take place? It was such problems as these that Tolstoy attempted to solve by reference to history (xii. 309, 313, 320). But Seeley has obviously not understood that Tolstoy strove to give 'straight answers' to these 'accursed questions'.

There is no need to dwell here in more detail on criticism of Tolstoy's conception of history, especially since, besides those who have rejected it, there are those who have attempted to evaluate its significance (V. Asmus, R. F. Christian, A. Saburov, E. Kupreyanova, E. Wasiolek).[13]

Without claiming any special authority as an interpreter of Tolstoy's philosophy of history, the present author offers the following brief statement of his views. Tolstoy's main idea concerns the dependence of historical circumstances on the coincidence of a countless number of causes. 'Without each of these causes nothing could have happened. So all of these causes—millions of causes—coincided in order to bring about that which happened' (xi. 4–5). The historical process, according

---

[11] F. F. Seeley, 'Tolstoy's Philosophy of History', in: *New Essays on Tolstoy*, ed. M. V. Jones (Cambridge, 1978), 179–82.

[12] L. N. Tolstoy, *Polnoe sobranie sochinenii v 90 tomakh* (M.–L., 1928–64), xii. 305 (henceforth referred to in the text by volume and page number).

[13] V. Asmus, 'Prichina i tsel' v istorii po romanu L. N. Tolstogo "Voina i mir"', in: *Iz istorii russkikh literaturnykh otnoshenii XVIII–XX vv.* (M.–L., 1959), 209; R. F. Christian, *Tolstoy's 'War and Peace': A Study* (Oxford, 1962), 80–94, 110; A. A. Saburov, *'Voina i mir' L. N. Tolstogo: Problematika i estetika* (M., 1959), 280–6; E. N. Kupreyanova: (i) *Estetika L. N. Tolstogo* (M., 1966), 192–200; (ii) 'O problematike i zhanrovoi prirode "Voiny i mira"', *Russkaya literatura*, 1985 no. 1, pp. 162–3; E. Wasiolek, *Tolstoy's Major Fiction* (Chicago–London, 1978), 117–27.

to Tolstoy, is a resultant force arising out of 'homogeneous, infinitely small elements, which control the masses'; and the homogeneous tendencies of men serve as these elements, which are 'the differentials of history' (xi. 265–7). The significance of the 'homogeneous tendencies of men' is reflected not only in the authorial digressions, but also in the episodes where Pierre is in captivity, in the shed for captive soldiers, where 'only now, for the first time Pierre came fully to appreciate the pleasure of food when he felt hungry, of drink when he felt thirsty, of sleep when he felt tired. The satisfaction of one's needs— good food, cleanliness, freedom—now that he was deprived of these things, seemed to Pierre to be perfect happiness . . .' (xii. 97–8).[14] The Tolstoyan model of history might be seen figuratively in the form of the movement of a crowd striving toward a certain tangible, simple goal—a crowd, for instance, that wants to receive food that is being distributed, or get on to public transport in the rush-hour. Let us recall how Tolstoy describes the movements of the French army before and after the battle of Borodino. Napoleon's soldiers, 'hungry, ragged and exhausted by the campaign, and in full view of an army which was barricading Moscow from them', went to fight 'in order to get food and rest as conquerors in Moscow' (xi. 219–20). This theme of 'swarm' movement occurs again in Tolstoy many years after *Voina i mir*, when he describes the movement of the crowd in the unfinished short story *Khodynka*: 'Emel'yan . . . rushed forward, . . . only because everyone else was rushing forward . . . Behind him, on both sides, there were people . . . That one aim, which he had from the very beginning set himself—to get to the tents and receive the sack full of gifts . . . drew him on . . .' (xxxviii. 208–9). The course of world events, according to Tolstoy, 'is determined from on high, depends on many arbitrary decisions of the people taking part in these events', and therefore 'the influence of a Napoleon on these people is only external and fictitious' (xi. 219).

These philosophical-historical reflections of Tolstoy were not only not 'alien to Bulgakov', but received direct reflection in his stage adaptation of *Voina i mir*. The Bulgakov version of *Voina i mir* features a narrator, and this narrator on several occasions refers to the Tolstoyan theme of the inevitability of historical events and the imaginary role of 'great men' in these events.

In 1812 the forces of Western Europe crossed the Russian borders and war began; that is, an event took place that is contrary to human reason and to all of human nature. Millions of men committed against one another such an endless number of crimes,

---

[14] The following words from Tolstoy—'In captivity, in the shed, Pierre recognized not with his mind but with his whole being' that happiness 'consists in satisfying one's basic human needs' (xii. 152)—were also intended by Bulgakov to be included in his adaptation, but he did not complete this section and crossed it out. Institute of Russian Literature of the Academy of Sciences of the USSR (Pushkin House), Leningrad (hereafter IRLI), *fond* 369, no. 207 (manuscript), *list* 66 *ob*.

frauds, treacheries, thefts, forgeries and issue of false banknotes, robberies, acts of arson and murder as would not find record in centuries in all the courts of the world, yet which those who committed them did not at the time regard as crimes.

With these words, corresponding to the beginning of the third volume of the novel (xi. 3), the narrator, in scene iv of Bulgakov's adaptation, introduces the theme of war.[15] And in the scene of the battle of Borodino (scene iii) there are Tolstoy's famous words about Napoleon: 'Even without his orders what he wanted was being done, and he once more gave orders only because orders were expected from him. And he once more submissively started to fulfil that sad inhuman role pre-destined for him' (cf. xi. 257). The stage adaptation also includes the no less famous characterization of Kutuzov's conduct after the French withdrawal from Moscow: 'from that time Kutuzov's activity consisted merely in holding back his troops, by means of power, cunning, and entreaties, from any pointless engagement with the [anyway] perishing foe' (scene xxiv; cf. xii. 113–14). Tolstoy's thoughts are expressed in the adaptation not only by the narrator, but also by Pierre Bezukhov ask-ing (as in the novel), as he is sent to be shot: 'But who then is doing this? Who?' (scene xxiii; cf. xii. 39–40).

In *Belaya gvardiya* the course of events is seen by Bulgakov in a similar light. Describing the conversations between the 'arrivals' from Moscow and Petersburg and the Kiev house-owner Vasilisa about Petlyura and the civil war in the Ukraine, the author notes: 'It was a myth. Petlyura was a myth. He never existed. It was a myth as remarkable as the myth about the non-existent Napoleon, but far less attractive' (B. 73). Bulgakov's words here bewilder students of his work. What connection has Petlyura with Napoleon? Levin tries to find the explanation for this parallel in the fact that, according to *Belaya gvardiya*, Petlyura was freed by the Hetman from cell no. 666. Levin links this 'number of the Beast' with Pierre Bezukhov's attempts to solve the riddle of Napoleon-Antichrist; he also refers to Petlyura's French-sounding Christian name—'Simón'.[16] Elendea Proffer makes the further point that the comparison of Petlyura with Napoleon 'reveals the degradation of the theme: Napoleon was a great world leader, Petliura is minor in com-parison'.[17] But, in fact, the Bulgakov parallel makes sense precisely in the Tolstoyan context. For Tolstoy and Bulgakov both Napoleon and Petlyura are myths not in the sense that they did not exist in reality, but in the sense that, as Tolstoy put it, 'the influence of these people is only external and fictive', and they are 'labels that give name to an event

[15] IRLI, *fond* 369, no. 207 (manuscript), *list* 10, *stranitsa* 19; no. 208 (typescript), *list* 17. Cf. A. Colin Wright, 'Mikhail Bulgakov's Adaptation of *War and Peace*', *Canadian-American Slavic Studies*, 1981 no. 5, p. 15; M. Bulgakov, *P'esy* (M., 1986), 553.

[16] Levin, op. cit. (n. 1), 322.

[17] Proffer, *Bulgakov* (n. 6), 152–3.

...'. 'All this is nonsense. If it hadn't been him it would have been another. And if not another—then someone else again'—the author (or his hero) says of Petlyura in *Belaya gvardiya* (B. 67). 'This Simon never even existed . . . He was simply a myth, born in the Ukraine in the mist of the terrible year 1918 . . .'. What then *was* there?

There was rabid hatred. There were four hundred thousand Germans, and around them fourfold forty times four hundred thousand peasants with hearts burning with unassuaged malice . . . And requisitioned horses, and confiscated grain, and fat-faced landlords returned to their estates under the Hetman, the quiver of hatred at the word 'officers' . . . And in the peasants' minds thoughts . . . of the need for that reform for which they had longed for centuries:

> All land to the peasants.
> Three hundred acres per man.
> No more landlords . . .   (B. 65)

In *Dni Turbinykh* this Tolstoyan conception of a 'swarm-like' inevitable historical movement, sweeping away the Hetman and the officers and then Petlyura himself, received expression above all in the words of Myshlaevsky when he calls the 'grandpa' (*did*) who said that all the young men of his village had run off to Petlyura a 'God-bearing', 'Tolstoyan old bastard'. But in the last act there is a change in the emotional colouring of this reference, which comes from the lips of the same Myshlaevsky. Refusing to participate afresh in the civil war, Myshlaevsky says 'it's God-bearing business now'.[18] 'God-bearing' precisely in the Tolstoyan sense: depending upon the conjunction of 'many arbitrary decisions of the people participating in these events' and, consequently, not subordinated to the will of one person, actions 'determined from on high'.

Tolstoy and Bulgakov recognized that movements and wars in which peoples engaged conformed to certain laws and were inevitable: in their view of history they were determinists. As many critics have observed, a deterministic view of history, as something 'predetermined from on high', linked Tolstoy with Hegel. But with this the similarity between them ended: the Hegelian worship of progress and its bearers, the worship of great historical personalities, was totally alien to Tolstoy. In opposing to 'a general and natural inevitability' a consciousness of freedom, innate to man despite this inevitability, Tolstoy followed not Hegel, but Kant (xxxv. 183; cf. xv. 235–46): 'Having proved incontrovertibly from the standpoint of reason the law of causality or necessity, Kant comes to recognize on this same path the *Intellegibele Wille*

[18] Cited according to the final revision of the play, prepared in 1940 and presented by E. S. Bulgakova in 1953 (Central State Archive of Literature and Art (TsGALI), Moscow, *fond* 2723, *opis'* 1, *ed. khr.* 468; IRLI, *fond* 369, no. 3). In the printed edition (M. A. Bulgakov, *P'esy 20-kh godov* (L., 1989), 113, 157), instead of 'God-bearing actions', one finds 'actions which are not ours'. Cf. M. Bulgakov, *Dramy i komedii* (M., 1965), 26 and 114.

(conscious will) which, as opposed to the sensible will, does not obey the law of causality and can exist alongside the general law of necessity.'[19] 'Without this conception of freedom', it is argued in *Voina i mir*, 'man would not only be unable to understand life, but he would be unable to live for a single moment.' Besides the question of history, man is also faced with the question of ethics: 'What is conscience and the consciousness of the good and evil of actions that result from the consciousness of freedom?' (xii. 324–5). How can and should a person behave who acts not as the subject of history, but as its object?

This question was of prime significance for Bulgakov too: it is put not only in *Belaya gvardiya* and *Dni Turbinykh*, but also in all his subsequent works. The main theme of *Mol'er* and *Poslednie dni* (*Pushkin*) (as also, to a significant extent, *Master i Margarita*) is the fate of a man living in the shadow of the inexorable power of history and the state. Adapting *Voina i mir* for the stage, Bulgakov reproduced not only the Tolstoyan idea of the inevitability of war, but also the view of war as an 'event contrary to reason and human nature'. And in this respect the finale of the adaptation was of particular importance—in the play, by contrast with the novel, Bulgakov had to express the main idea of the work not in an elaborate epilogue, but by dramatic action.

In the final scene of Bulgakov's play the French officer Ramballe, frost-bitten during the retreat, and his batman Morel come upon some Russian soldiers by their camp-fire; the soldiers feed Morel with *kasha* and try to imitate the song which Morel sings. 'They're people too', says one of the soldiers, and once again the voice of the Narrator breaks in: 'And everything fell silent. The stars, as if they knew that no one would see them now, began to disport themselves in the black sky. Now bursting into flame, now fading, now flickering, they busily whispered among themselves about some joyful but secret thing' (scene xxx; cf. xii. 194–6). What is the meaning of this finale? In the only article devoted to Bulgakov's version of *Voina i mir*, Levin has voiced the opinion that the finale of the adaptation 'was possibly dictated by political causes. The fraternization of the simple Russian soldiers with their French comrades in misfortune may be interpreted in the sense of the international solidarity of the proletariat.'[20] Such an explanation, reducing Bulgakov to the level of a conformist hack playwright, like Dymogatsky in *Bagrovyi ostrov*, is entirely unfounded. First and foremost, Levin disregards the fact that the whole of this scene, from the first to the last word, belongs to Tolstoy and occupies in *Voina i mir* a by no means incidental, but, in fact, an exceptionally important place. It presents us with the *Weltanschauung* that has been formed in the course of the novel and found reflection in those episodes where

---

[19] Cf. Kupreyanova, 'O problematike' (n. 13), 166.
[20] Levin, op. cit. (n. 1), 333.

Nikolay Rostov experiences 'joyful delight' during a conversation with a German peasant ('und Vivat die ganze Welt', ix. 155–6), and where the Russian and French soldiers laugh amicably together in the picket lines on the eve of Austerlitz (ix. 213–14). Further reflections on these questions led Tolstoy to the conviction that 'to prefer one's own nation and state to all other nations and other states' 'was and is to this day the source of the greatest disasters of mankind' (xxxix. 50–74; 70–1, 519–20; xc. 48–53, 425–31).

Did Bulgakov, too, come to this Tolstoyan idea? And, in general, what was the nature of Tolstoy's influence on his work? Bulgakov was undoubtedly not a writer of the 'Tolstoyan school' (if one accepts the existence of such a 'school' after Tolstoy). The obvious ancestor of Bulgakov in Russian classical literature is Gogol'. This was noted already by Bulgakov's first biographer and critic, his friend P. S. Popov. 'The main advantage of *Dead Souls* in comparison with Dostoevsky and Tolstoy, in particular the latter, is Gogol''s humour and his ability to enter into a direct relationship with the reader', he remarked in one of his letters.[21] There is no doubt that the same ability 'to enter into a direct relationship with a reader' was characteristic of Bulgakov too.

The work of Bulgakov that is closest to Tolstoy is *Belaya gvardiya*. Writing of the play *Dni Turbinykh* (based on *Belaya gvardiya*, to which his remarks therefore may also apply), Popov attempted to understand what determined the 'soft lyrical colouring' of Bulgakov's depiction of the Turbin house:

Perhaps it is embodied in the symbolism of the cream-coloured blinds, or of the Christmas tree, or of the heavenly curtain studded with stars—but there is here some all-subduing stimulus of life, and this is what acts so powerfully that it pulls together all the parts. It is like the symbol of the epoch of *War and Peace*:

> What is stronger than death and fate?
> A sweet Ankovsky pie plumb on a plate.[22]

The theme of home, the family, of family comfort, very important for *Voina i mir*, is indeed one of the main motifs of *Belaya gvardiya* and *Dni Turbinykh*. With good reason the former pre-war cosiness is remembered in the novel with such poignant force, a poignancy which in its turn is linked with *Voina i mir*: 'the bronze lamp under the lampshade, the finest bookcases in the world full of books, smelling of mysterious chocolate, with Natasha Rostova, with the Captain's daughter . . .' (B. 15). But Tolstoy's attitude towards the 'Ankovsky pie' (the favourite pie of his wife's parents—named after N. B. Anke, a friend of the

[21] Undated letter of May 1932. IRLI, *fond* 369, no. 466. Cf. Ya. S. Lur'e, 'Iz perepiski M. A. Bulgakova s V. V. Veresaevym i P. S. Popovym', forthcoming in the journal *Russkaya literatura*.

[22] Letter of 1 July 1934. IRLI, *fond* 369, no. 466. The couplet is quoted from Tolstoy. See I. Tolstoy, *Moi vospominaniya* (M., 1933), 98. Cf. Lur'e, 'Iz perepiski' (n. 21).

household) changed sharply in the course of the writer's life. Gradually, according to Tolstoy's son Sergey L'vovich, this pie became for Tolstoy 'the emblem of a particular *Weltanschauung*', namely, faith in the stability of material well-being and 'an unbending conviction of the stability of the present order of things'.[23] 'The muted struggle against the Ankovsky pie not only does not end, it is growing, and the crashings of the earthquake tearing the pie to pieces are already audible here and there', Tolstoy wrote to T. A. Kuz'minskaya (lxiii. 291; cf. lxxxiii, no. 82, p. 68).

Unlike Tolstoy, Bulgakov had very direct experience of the 'crashings of the earthquake tearing the pie to pieces'; he was aware also of the reasons for this 'earthquake', but the earthquake evoked in him not joy, but rather nostalgia for a comfortable way of life, a table with a pie, and 'cream-coloured blinds'. Of course, in Bulgakov too the theme of the 'Ankovsky pie' later acquired a different meaning: in *Master i Margarita* the 'Torgsin' store and the luxurious restaurant of Griboedov House, carefully protected against the frequenters of communal kitchens, aroused in him no sympathy. But this attitude came much later, in the 1930s, while in *Belaya gvardiya* the memory of the 'earthquake' was all too fresh in his mind. In the letter to the Soviet Government in 1930 Bulgakov, alongside his statement of loyalty to the traditions of *Voina i mir*, declares that his ideal is 'beloved and Great Evolution'.

Neither did Bulgakov share the Tolstoyan worship of the peasant in Platon Karataev; in his depiction of country life (in *Zapiski yunogo vracha*) he is much closer to Chekhov and Bunin. Nor could he accept the Tolstoyan idea of 'non-resistance to evil'. On the contrary, the reaction of his heroes to the violence and brutality of Petlyura's supporters is to some extent opposed to Tolstoyan non-resistance to evil. After witnessing these atrocities, Doctor Turbin (in the original finale of *Belaya gvardiya*) passionately dreams of finding a 'naval revolver' in his hand: 'He aims. At the head. One gets it . . . In the head. A second . . .', and then, returning home, he weeps and reproaches himself precisely for his inability to act in this way: 'A fine one I am! Useless intelligentsia scum . . .'.[24] Faced with the civil war, which in the Ukraine was largely nationalist in character, Bulgakov was scarcely able to reject with the same determination as Tolstoy 'the preference for one's own nation' against all others and stand firmly above the Ukrainian–Russian conflict, as V. G. Korolenko was able to do in those years.

Nevertheless, one particular feature of Tolstoy's outlook was pro-

[23] S. L. Tolstoy, 'Yumor v razgovorakh L. N. Tolstogo', in: *Tolstoy: Pamyatniki tvorchestva i zhizni* (M., 1920), ii. 12–14.
[24] M. Bulgakov, 'Konets Petlyury', *Avrora*, 1968 no. 12, pp. 97–9.

foundly shared by Bulgakov, and for both writers it was highly important: historical necessity does not deprive a man of his sense of individual freedom—it does not affect his 'conscience and consciousness of
good and evil'.

A description of the stars shining above a world gripped by war was
used by Bulgakov to end not only his adaptation of *Voina i mir*, but also
his *Belaya gvardiya*, written some years before. Let us recall the end of
Bulgakov's novel. On the approaches to Kiev the armoured train
'Proletarian' has halted; a sentry guards it, a sentry as frozen as the
soldiers in *Voina i mir*. The people in the city sleep and dream. The
small boy Pet'ka Shcheglov dreams of a shining diamond globe that
showers him with droplets. The night goes on. 'During the second half
of the night the whole heavy dark blueness, God's curtain drawn over
the world, became covered with stars.' The cross on the statue of
Vladimir seems like a sword. 'But the sword is not to be feared. Everything will pass ... The sword will vanish, but the stars will remain,
when not even a shadow of our bodies and deeds remains on earth.
There is not a single person alive who does not know this. Why then are
we unwilling to turn our gaze towards the stars? Why?' (B. 266–7, 269–
70). If we go back to *Voina i mir*, we find there not only stars, but also a
ball consisting of moving drops. This ball is seen by Pierre Bezukhov in
a dream, just as happens to his young namesake in Bulgakov. 'An
old, gentle Swiss teacher' exhibits the globe:

A live, oscillating ball ... The whole surface of the ball consisted of drops tightly
pressed together. And these drops moved, shifted ...
   'That is life,' said the old teacher. (xii. 158)

The metaphoric significance of the end of *Belaya gvardiya* is obvious.
War, which is inevitable but also contrary to 'human nature', is
'torment, blood, hunger and plague', while, in counterbalance, there is
the metaphor of life: the shining diamond ball, not accessible to grown-
ups, but placed in the hands of a child. And, finally, the stars. The
image of the starry sky constantly occurs in *Voina i mir*—not just in the
scene by the camp-fire, but in earlier chapters too: Pierre sees the starry
sky (and the comet of 1812) after his first declaration of love to Natasha
(whose relationship with Andrey has just ended) (x. 372; this excerpt is
included by Bulgakov in his adaptation), then again in Moscow after
the intimate conversation with Ramballe (xi. 374), and again, walking
with the column of prisoners and laughing at the captivity of his
'immortal soul' (xii.105–6). So what, then, is the symbolic significance
of the stars in Tolstoy and Bulgakov? 'Two things fill my soul with a
constantly new and increasing wonder and awe and they do so the
more, the oftener and more attentively that I reflect on them: the starry
sky above me and the moral law within me.' These words of Kant were

always remembered by Tolstoy and they were used by him as the epigraph to his tract *O zhizni* (xxvi. 313).[25] Bulgakov remembered them too—for it is this very same idea of the 'restless old fellow Immanuel' that figures in Voland's conversation with Berlioz at Chistye prudy (B. 429).

The starry sky was both for Tolstoy and for Bulgakov the symbol and embodiment of the 'moral law' within man. Tolstoy set against the worship of historical progress, inherent in both Hegel and the positivists, the sense of a firmly established human moral duty (xxxv. 183). It appears that Bulgakov's views were similar. As I. Vinogradov has observed, the essence of the philosophical-historical conception of *Master i Margarita* may be reduced to one single principle: 'be true to yourself, to your convictions . . . Even if the whole world is collapsing all around. And even if no one can give guarantee that the kingdom of truth and justice will one day triumph . . .'.[26]

[25] I. Kant, *Kritika prakticheskogo razuma*, comp. N. Smirnov (Spb., 1879), 190. Cf. I. Kant, *Sochineniya v shesti tomakh* (M., 1965), iv, ch. 1, 499.
[26] I. Vinogradov, 'Zaveshchanie mastera', *Voprosy literatury*, 1968 no. 6, p. 54.

Alexis Aladin: The Last Years
(1920–1927)

By R. F. CHRISTIAN

In the long chronicle of Russian romantic exiles, the name of Alexis Aladin deserves honourable mention. Having fled from Russia in 1897 after imprisonment for suspected political subversion, he spent three years in France and Belgium before arriving in London as a penniless refugee in 1900. Five years later he took advantage of a political amnesty to return to Russia, where he rapidly rose to fame as the leader of the Trudovik Party in the First Russian Duma. After the dissolution of the Duma he found himself back in England, where he lived until 1917. In the spring of that year he went (or was sent) back to his native country under British auspices and, after being implicated in the Kornilov rising and imprisoned by the Bolsheviks, he joined the Volunteer Army and took an active part in the fighting in the south of Russia before eventually joining General Vrangel''s staff in the Crimea in 1920. In the late summer of 1920 he reappeared in London as Vrangel''s spokesman in the dying days of the Russian Civil War.[1] While officially representing the Armed Forces of South Russia, he wore the uniform of a British army officer, and continued to do so for the next year, long after Vrangel''s defeat, as the guest of the British Government, living at the National Liberal Club near Whitehall as a temporary foreign member and hoping that his Russian background and his services to Britain would qualify him for some worthwhile temporary employment until the situation in his native land became clearer. Although he had lost all contact with his wife and family in Russia, he was not without friends in Britain, in particular the Scottish businessman, David Russell, and Miss Constance Nightingale, a Quaker schoolmistress at (and later headmistress of) the Mount School, York, whom he had met on his return to England from Constantinople in 1920. For the next few years until his death in 1927 Aladin kept up a monumental exchange of letters with these two friends, and it is primarily on the basis of this unpublished correspondence,[2] together with other archive material in the Manchester and St

---

[1] See my 'Alexis Aladin, Trudovik Leader in the First Duma: Materials for a Biography (1873–1920)', *Oxford Slavonic Papers*, NS xxi (1988), 131–52.
[2] The letters are now in the John Rylands Library, University of Manchester (hereafter referred to as JRL), where they have been listed chronologically and stored in six boxes. The addressees are

Andrews University Libraries, that an attempt will be made in this article to reconstruct the last years of the life of this exceptionally versatile, but tragically unfulfilled anglophile Russian *émigré*.

1

For the first few months of his third sojourn in Britain Aladin was in a reasonably buoyant mood. He held the rank of major in the British army, enjoyed the hospitality of a fashionable London club, and was sought after for his views on Anglo-Russian relations and the Russian Civil War. Nevertheless, in 1920 he was already writing to Russell bemoaning his penniless condition and appealing to him for financial help. Shortly afterwards the need to establish himself and his finances on a secure basis became more urgent as a result of a chance meeting on a Channel steamer bound for France with a beautiful young American woman of seventeen. The Hon. Clare Boothe Luce's recollections of their meeting and subsequent brief, but close, friendship have been coloured by the passage of time. In an article published in 1960[3] she recalled how 'Colonel' Alexis Aladin used his hypnotic eyes and voice to cure her of seasickness while travelling from England to France on an exceptionally stormy winter's day in what she mistakenly referred to as 1922. Mrs Luce described him, nearly forty years after the event, as not handsome, with a leathery-looking face, shaggy eyebrows and a rough clipped moustache. 'I remember that I didn't like him', she observed, and went on to say that he subsequently called at her Paris *pension* at breakfast-time, showed her his cigarette case with the signature of Nicholas II, and made the astonishing claim that he personally had rescued the Tsar's *eldest* daughter, Grand Duchess Ol'ga, in Ekaterinburg in July 1918 and had sent her with friends to Vladivostok from where she escaped abroad. Mrs Luce stated in her article that she never saw Aladin again after their brief meeting at the breakfast table, but Aladin's letters tell a different story. There is no doubt that he met Clare Boothe on numerous occasions between January and March 1921, in both Paris and London, that she was temporarily infatuated by him, and that the possibility of marriage was discussed. In February he wrote to Russell about 'new horizons' in his private life, and sent him a press cutting of Miss Boothe, 'voted the most beautiful girl on the Riviera in the recent contest held here at Nice'.[4] But on 9 April 1921 he wrote disconsolately 'my girl—she is

hereafter referred to as DR (Sir David Russell, 1872–1956) and CN (Miss Constance Nightingale, 1892–1967).

[3] *McCall's Magazine*, pt. 1 (May 1960) and pt. 2 (June 1960).
[4] DR, 6 Feb. 1921.

mine in many senses, so let me call her that—has gone to America
[. . .]. She is beyond my reach and help.' She continued to write to him
from America, but her numerous letters and photographs which
chance to have survived are not at present available to the public,[5] while
his side of the correspondence was most likely destroyed.

Aladin was deeply depressed by his inability to find paid work in
Britain and told Russell that he had briefly contemplated suicide, but
was restrained by the thought that such action might seem to be connected with the failure of his relationship with Clare Boothe. Although
still in army uniform, he despaired of being offered any suitable
employment in London, and suggested to Russell that he should
change into mufti and undertake an expedition to the Baltic States,
Poland, and Czechoslovakia. He even wrote to John Buchan, whom he
greatly admired, asking him to raise the necessary funds for such an
expedition, but if there was a reply it must have been unfavourable. He
then contemplated returning to Russia and obtained an interview with
L. B. Krasin, the Soviet trade representative, only to be told that there
was no possibility of allowing him to go back to Moscow.[6] It is not clear
what financial benefit he derived from 'being a guest of the British
Government',[7] but it was doubtless humiliating for him to be constantly short of money and to have to rely on frequent cheques from
Russell and the hospitality of friends who took him to concerts and
ballets in London. Like more famous émigrés before him, however, he
found free shelter in the Reading Room of the British Museum, where
his horizons were extended to include India, Egypt, and Chaldea. His
reading ranged widely over the fields of history, literature, religion,
physics, and mathematics, and it was not long before he also resumed
writing, both on current affairs (especially the situation in Russia) and
on his early childhood days. He cherished an ambition to make the
British people better acquainted with Russian poetry, and to this end
persuaded Miss Nightingale to improve and put into verse his own
translations of poems by Aleksey Tolstoy, Maikov, and Nekrasov.
Through the good offices of an American lady[8] he came into contact
with the millionaire mining engineer, art collector, and philanthropist
Chester Beatty, and for several months in 1922 he lived at Beatty's
luxurious town house in Kensington Palace Gardens and at his country
residence in Kent, assisting him in his search for rare manuscripts and
enjoying a standard of living he had never known before; but the
friendship between the two men cooled off, partly, according to Miss

[5] Deposited in St Andrews University Library. They cannot be consulted until 1994.

[6] The interview took place at the beginning of June 1921 and is referred to in a letter to CN,
dated 4 June 1921.

[7] CN, 27 Sept. 1921.

[8] See Professor R. H. Freeborn's edited notes (dated July 1967) of a visit to CN in May 1967
(filed with the Aladin papers in the JRL).

Nightingale, because of Aladin's unwillingness to accept a poorly remunerated post elsewhere. What he really wanted was to obtain work as a journalist, and he asked Russell to approach the *Scotsman* on his behalf, but Russell's intercession was evidently fruitless, and his own approaches to *The Times*, the *Morning Post*, the *Daily Mail*, and the *Manchester Guardian* were equally unsuccessful. He did publish two political articles in the *Evening Standard* and a short piece in the *English Review* in 1922, but his prospects of ever establishing himself as a journalist for a British newspaper or periodical were minimized by his eccentric English syntax and quaintly bookish phraseology, despite his ability to write fluently in his adopted language on a great variety of subjects from the most popular to the most abstruse. Meanwhile he continued to send Miss Nightingale his prose translations of more Russian poets, including Zhukovsky and Nadson, and to revise some earlier versions by English friends of stories by Korolenko, for whom he had a lifelong affection.

The year 1922 found Aladin living in bed-sitters in Hampstead and Gower Street in severely straitened circumstances. By now he had become an active member of The Quest, a religious and spiritual society which sought 'to promote enquiry into the nature of religious and other supranormal experiences and the means of testing their value'. It also published a journal of the same name, under the editorship at the time of G. R. S. Mead, which invited contributions on 'the comparative study of religion, philosophy and science'. Aladin was a regular attender at its meetings and lectured to its members in June 1923 on 'The Way of Unity, where Mind and Love are united'.[9] His letters contain extensive summaries and criticisms of the numerous papers and discussions he heard there by such distinguished speakers as Mead, Jessie West, Sir Lawrence Jones, and Florence Ayscough, and references to his own participation in experimental psychical research. *The Quest* published his article 'Ikhnaton and Bolshevism' in April 1923 and, although this was his only major contribution,[10] he continued to read the journal regularly until a few days before his death. His earnest preoccupation with spiritual problems, however, could do nothing to satisfy his pressing material needs. He tried unsuccessfully to renew his wartime connections with the War Office and the Foreign Office. He contemplated a short visit to Germany 'to observe and report',[11] but there was nobody to finance it. He showed some of his writings to Sir Hall Caine, who made encouraging remarks about his style, but without any commitment. More promisingly, he received

---

[9] DR, 15 June 1921.

[10] Other contributions to *The Quest* were 'The Sphinx Riddle', xiv (Oct. 1922–July 1923), 541–3; 'A Page from Life', xv (Oct. 1923–July 1924), 248–54; and 'The Three Symbols in the Hands of Osiris', ibid. 524–6.

[11] CN, 11 Aug. 1923.

an invitation to go to Prague from a Czech officer, General Kleçanda, whom he had met as a junior officer in a Bolshevik prison in Bykhov in 1917 and who had now risen to a senior position of command in the Czech capital. As a first step he approached some British firms, on whose behalf he felt he could do business in Prague, but his overtures were unsuccessful. His request to Russell, however, to allow him to represent his paper interests in Czechoslovakia, Bulgaria, and Yugoslavia got a favourable response, and in October 1923 he seemed to be on the point of leaving Britain in the unhappy belief that there was no future for him there, that he was regarded with suspicion by certain sections of British officialdom, and was at times deliberately snubbed at Anglo-Russian receptions to which he had been officially invited—the consequences, no doubt, of the questionable role he had played as a Russian in British uniform fighting in Russia during the Civil War. But the long-awaited visa for Prague had still not arrived when in November 1923 Aladin's private life was further complicated by the imminent birth of his only child. 'I have acquired a new responsibility', he wrote to Russell in July. 'A woman met me, a house maid by her situation, a brave soul by her nature [. . .]. Now she tells me that she may become the mother of my child.'[12] Although they were never officially married, Aladin always regarded the lady as his wife, and referred to her as Mrs Florence Aladin in his will. Aladin and 'the mother', as he usually called her in his correspondence, were an ill-matched couple, but they stayed together for the rest of Aladin's life and he proved to be a proud and devoted father. His son, also called Alexis, was born on 23 December: 'for him a rebirth', as Aladin put it with his belief in reincarnation, 'after a short stay in the realm of beyond'.[13] About the same time Aladin began to write a long series of letters to Miss Nightingale, recalling to the best of his memory the events of his childhood and youth, which he hoped would form an autobiography set against the background of contemporary Russian life. These letters in a slightly edited form were subsequently published under the title 'A Childhood' in the *Rothmill Quarterly*,[14] the house journal of Russell's paper mill, and constitute a prelude to the unpublished (and for stylistic reasons largely unpublishable) semi-factual, semi-fictional 'pages from life', which he had written for Russell earlier in 1923, and which mainly concern his adult life in England and his adventures in Russia during the Civil War.

By the end of September 1924 his arrangements to visit Prague were complete and he set off via Paris with a mixture of British and Russian soil (he had brought the latter to England with him in 1920) wrapped

[12] DR, 15 July 1923.
[13] DR, 24 Dec. 1923.
[14] Published in seven parts in vols. xxvi (1954–5) and xxvii (1955–6).

up in a handwritten copy of Psalm 91. His time in Paris was brief, but enjoyable. He 'communed', he said, with 'the unseen reality' in Notre Dame, paid homage in the Panthéon to the distinguished French aviator Guinemar, whose photograph he had taken back to Russia with him in 1917, re-established contact with his friend the Russian poet Yury Terapiano ('ex-Gnostic and cabalist', as he called him), whom he took with him, under some duress, to the Madeleine to pray, and called on his 'old friend' Countess M. N. Chernysheva-Bezobrazova, a 'grand Russian lady' employed at the time on the Diamond Exchange in Paris.[15] He arrived in Prague in early October, was modestly accommodated by a Czech friend and left to his own devices. It is difficult to discover precisely what his work there involved, although to judge from his extensive correspondence he had ample time for sightseeing and reading. One purpose of his visit was to float the idea of the formation by appropriate Czech organizations of a Russian Cossack and Peasant Bank which could provide credits for trading with Soviet Russia, but it is not clear what progress his overtures made. He applied for membership of the Russian Section of the International Agrarian Bureau set up in Prague under the auspices of the leader of the local Agrarian Party, and his application was accepted. He gave two lectures in the Czech capital on the Russian peasantry and agrarian problems, and attended one by P. N. Milyukov in the course of which he heard himself referred to as a political adventurer, whereupon 'I got up, said thank you and walked out'.[16] By late November the possibility of extending his visit or of obtaining any remunerative work seemed remote, and he was forced to conclude: 'My work in Prague is finished; quite successful in one respect, deeply invigorating and instructive in another, it is a partial failure in so far as my concrete proposal is concerned'[17] (a reference, perhaps, to the projected Cossack and Peasant Bank). During his two months' stay money had been a constant source of worry, despite several successful appeals to Russell and Miss Nightingale, whose periodic cheques were gratefully acknowledged.

As his time in Czechoslovakia drew to a close, he received a letter from Russell[18] saying that the Department of Overseas Trade believed that there was a possibility of doing business in Bulgaria in blotting-papers and enclosing a list of likely buyers. Aladin suggested that he might travel home via Sofia and Belgrade in the hope of establishing a permanent link in Bulgaria and Yugoslavia for Russell's paper mill, and asked for hotel and travelling expenses. A cheque duly arrived and the trip took place, but Aladin was obliged to report that the prospects for trade in paper were not bright. The last week in December found him in a hotel in Paris with no money. Once again he had to appeal to

Russell for living expenses and to Miss Nightingale for his fare home. His invitation to her to join him in Paris for a few days was not accepted, and he returned to England for the New Year with the firm intention of going on to America in February to continue the work begun in Prague. He told Russell that he wished to go to America in order to put Russian and American farmers in contact with each other and to raise funds to continue the education of Russians in Czechoslovakia and organize estates in or near that country where Russians with an agricultural training could work until they were wanted in Russia.[19] Nobody in Russia, he added, would refuse to recognize that he was the first peasant leader on a national scale; but for reasons he had never understood he was debarred in England from any direct action in support of a cause so vital, he believed, to the interests of both countries. He needed £550 for his proposed campaign abroad, which would include travel to Paris, Prague, and Rome, as well as America.[20] Jan Masaryk, whom he had met previously in London, gave him official introductions to Czech consulates and legations in America, describing him as 'a serious and practical person'[21] with valuable connections there, and tentative arrangements were made for him to travel to America in June with Masaryk's father-in-law, Charles Crane. Permission arrived too late, however, and Crane left without him.

During the difficult summer of 1925 Aladin recalled nostalgically the days when he had worked for the Foreign Office and the War Office and had felt himself a man. He could not understand why the British preferred to deal with Kerensky and Savinkov rather than himself. He was after all 'half-British'.[22] At times he complained of the 'wilderness of loneliness' in London, his precarious situation, and the holes in his clothes. Yet he was too proud to accept the offer of some translation work 'for a few coppers',[23] although he did earn occasional fees from the Pathfinder organization, which employed people to trace references in the British Museum and elsewhere and to act as guides. Cheques continued to come in frequently, however, from his two loyal friends, and for a short time he wrote his letters on good-quality notepaper with the printed heading *Alexis Aladin, Ex-Member, The Duma, Russia.*

For all his disappointments Aladin was a man of great resilience, rarely disposed to self-pity. He wrote innumerable letters, or articles in letter form, in response to Russell's requests for his views on such diverse subjects as the training of leaders, the philosophy of Heraclitus, and the nature of the soul. He continued to play an active part in the proceedings of the Quest Society. He also attended a meeting of the newly founded Society for Cultural Relations with the Soviet Union,

[19] DR, 11 Jan. 1925.   [20] DR, 23 Jan. 1925.   [21] Letter of 14 May 1925.
[22] DR, 17 May 1925.   [23] CN, 29 June 1925.

where he heard J. M. Keynes address an audience including Bertrand Russell and H. G. Wells on the need for closer *rapprochement* with Russia. He found Keynes 'promising' but immature, handicapped by a pronounced insularity and a lack of first-hand revolutionary experience.[24] Nevertheless he felt that the Society deserved to be supported and approved of the chairman's desire to keep all channels of communication with Russia open.

The year 1926 saw a determined effort by Aladin to earn a living as a journalist or a businessman. His numerous published and unpublished political articles of this date are, despite their infelicitous expression, not without interest, and they will be referred to later; but as a source of income they were woefully inadequate. Even less remunerative were his forays into the business world. Aladin (an inveterate cigarette smoker) was briefly employed in the tobacco industry, but this did not produce the required results. More auspicious initially was his plan to co-operate with a Russian colonel living in Paris, an enterprising doll manufacturer who was visiting London with a Cossack choir. The intention was to create a line of British national dolls, painted wooden toys, and good-quality children's overcoats, made in France and sold in Britain by people interested in 'resurrecting the submerged art of simplicity and beauty'.[25] Discussions took place in London and ideas were exchanged, but the colonel was obliged to return to Paris unexpectedly and nothing came of the scheme. Soon afterwards Aladin became involved with a group of Russian gold-mine speculators and went to great lengths to absorb a mass of detail about the mining industry. However, his 'business adventures', as he called them, in this field did not prosper, and he was soon commenting sadly on castles in the air becoming castles in the sand.

Severely straitened circumstances and the lack of employment, however, did not mean that Aladin was cut off from London social life. Several invitations from Mayfair addresses, some addressed to General Aladin, requested the pleasure of his company for lunch or Christmas dinner. The programme of the City of London Debating Society for 1926–7 includes the entry 'General Alexis Aladin on Bolshevism: a debate opened by General Aladin on the proposition "That Bolshevism is not conducive to the happiness or prosperity of the Russian people"'.[26] His address book for 1926[27] contains some distinguished names and telephone numbers, including those of Mrs Chester Beatty, Winston Churchill, John Buchan, Lady Egerton, Lady Low, the Hon. Evelyn Hubbard, Sir Edward Hulton, and several other residents of London WC1 and SW3. On the other hand, complaints begin to multiply in his correspondence about his humiliating treatment at the

[24] DR, 4 Nov. 1925.   [25] CN, 14 Jan. 1926.   [26] JRL, Box 28.   [27] JRL, Box 27.

hands of the British Government. He was, he said, 'caged up in Hampstead', ostracized, and reduced at times to eating one orange and smoking a quarter of a cigarette a day. But despite all hardships and humiliations he continued to believe that his work abroad in promoting the cause of the Russian peasantry would contribute, however marginally, to his ideal of the eventual establishment of a peasant-based economy in Russia. His touching faith in the innate superiority of the Russian agricultural labourer sustained him in the face of further rebuffs from an ungrateful British Government which failed to appreciate his diagnoses of the political and economic situation in Russia. In January 1927 a letter from the Foreign Office regretted that there was 'no opportunity at present of utilising your services',[28] and that appears to have ended his attempts to re-establish old links with his former employers.

The last few months of Aladin's life were marred by almost constant ill health. Details of his own physical condition occupy much more space in his correspondence than before, although not to the exclusion of some pertinent comments on Russian and Chinese political affairs and the many religious, philosophical, and scientific books which continued to stimulate his enquiring mind. His last six weeks were spent in St Thomas's Hospital, London (with financial support from Miss Nightingale), where he tried hard to participate in the daily life of the ward despite his 'outlandish origin and bookish language'.[29] A fortnight before his death he wrote two long letters[30] expounding his views on J. W. Dunne's *An Experiment with Time*. The day before his final operation was due he was reading J. F. Ferrier's *Lectures on Greek Philosophy*. In his last letter to Miss Nightingale[31] he voiced his fears for the future of his only child. His words did not go unheeded and Miss Nightingale brought the young Alexis up as her own son. His death in a flying accident during the Second World War was a blow from which she never fully recovered.

Aladin died on 30 July 1927, aged 54, and was buried as requested in his British army officer's uniform. The headstone of his grave was designed, ordered, and paid for by Russell, who also shared in the expenses of the young Aladin's education and gave him a second home in Scotland. The obituary notices in *The Times* and the *Manchester Guardian* emphasized his mystical temperament, his hatred of materialism, his love of England, and his belief that the future of his native country lay with the peasantry. 'His influence will remain', said *The Times*, 'if only because he had undying faith in the cooperation between this country and the new Russia for which he desired to labour.'[32]

[28] JRL, Box 27.   [29] CN, 24 June 1927.   [30] To Mrs Queen, JRL, Box 6.
[31] CN, 22 July 1927.   [32] *The Times*, 5 Aug. 1927.

2

Aladin's colourful, unconventional, but basically sad and poignant life justifies a full biography. Such a biography would need to concentrate particularly on the political, religious, and scientific ideas he expressed in his later years. The second half of this article will concentrate on his political pronouncements.

If in his student days Aladin had displayed radical tendencies and an overt hostility towards the tsarist government (without ever countenancing terrorism), his long sojourn in England bred in him a profound respect for British-style constitutional monarchy and, indeed, for the British Empire as an institution. His fierce pride in being Russian was almost matched by his love of wearing British army uniform and his loyalty to the British War Office and the Foreign Office. His return to Russia in 1917 had the blessing of Lord Milner, and his active service under Denikin and Vrangel' placed him firmly in the White camp long before Vrangel' sent him to Europe in 1920 to plead his cause. Once resettled in London, Aladin lent his name to a White Russian programme entitled 'The Future of Russia',[33] which envisaged the creation of a united democratic political front incorporating all anti-Bolshevik elements both inside and outside Russia. Russians living abroad would be organized into groups, with Paris as a major centre, under the long-term aegis of an elected representative body and in the short term under the leadership of an experienced and trusted colleague, while effective liaison between them and their counterparts in Russia would be established and maintained by means unspecified in the document. All people interested in the programme were invited to contact Aladin at the National Liberal Club, and there is little doubt that at the time (in late 1920 or early 1921) he expected the early collapse of Bolshevik power. There is not the slightest evidence that he ever entertained Communist sympathies, despite suspicions to the contrary in certain British official quarters, and he remained consistently hostile to the political and economic theory and practice of Marxism. And yet, once it became clear that the Bolshevik Government was not going to collapse, he never became identified with any anti-communist group or policy abroad. Kerensky, who had been his opponent in the abortive Kornilov affair, understandably shunned him in exile. Milyukov and his Cadet friends mistrusted him as a political adventurer. He himself had no sympathy for the Grand Duke Cyril and his Monarchist group in Paris or for their supporters in London, and never wished to see the Romanov dynasty restored. Nevertheless, the Foreign Office, which was hardly well disposed to the

[33] Typescript in JRL, Box 9.

new regime in Russia, seemed reluctant to employ him in any capacity, perhaps because of his attempts to establish connections with Soviet representatives in London with a view to returning to Russia, or his eagerness to forge commercial and diplomatic relations with the Soviet Government. While abhorring Bolshevik cruelty and abuse of power, he was not averse in principle to a 'Soviet-style' structure of representation and administration, and once the Civil War was over he was enough of a realist not to expect the imminent downfall of the Communist regime forecast by some Western European politicians and journalists. To left-wing Russian *émigrés* Aladin seemed to have betrayed the cause he once apparently espoused; to right-wing official circles in Britain he appeared still to harbour pro-Russian sentiments. But, for all the apparent ambiguity of his position, he never betrayed his fundamental and almost mystical belief in the Russian peasantry and their vital role in the future prosperity of his country. If he was at times tempted to enquire about returning to Soviet Russia, it was not because of any political change of heart, but only because he thought he could be of use to the peasant cause. He was a founder member of the so-called Peasants' Union (*Krest'yanskii soyuz*) set up in the Crimea in 1920, the main aim of which was to develop the Russian economy on the basis of peasant smallholdings, to unite the peasantry on grounds of economic interest, to subordinate political to economic considerations and therefore to remain a non-party organization, and to raise the educational and cultural level of those who worked on the land. The founder members envisaged a pyramidal administrative structure, with local and regional cells sending elected representatives to a central Soviet, but their ambitious plans were soon frustrated by the destruction of Vrangel''s forces in the south of Russia. A year before this happened, however, in the autumn of 1920, Aladin was interviewed by a Reuters correspondent on the subject of Vrangel''s position and prospects, and spoke, incidentally, of the role of the new Peasants' Union.[34] Vrangel', he argued, had from a military point of view already performed a miracle. Politically he had initiated a series of radical reforms for the benefit of the largest, agricultural, section of the population, and his aims were to provide land for the peasants, self-government for the people, and home rule for the Cossack territories. The Peasants' Union was already delivering grain to Marseilles in exchange for British goods without any special trade agreement. British firms had their representatives in Constantinople. Vrangel''s troops were entering the Donets coal basin and before long would have enough coal for their own needs with some to spare for export. Trade prospects were good, but help was urgently needed.

A month later Aladin was present as Vrangel''s spokesman at a

[34] Typescript record of interview in JRL, Box 9.

conference on Anglo-Russian trade held at the offices of the Federation
of British Industries in London to consider setting up a limited
company in Britain to restore Russian rail and water transport, repair
Russian industry, supply Russian markets, and import Russian raw
materials needed by British industry. However, the unexpectedly rapid
collapse of the White armies put all such schemes temporarily in abey-
ance as the West faced up to the reality of the devastating Russian
famine of 1921.

In August 1921 Aladin wrote a long letter to Lord Robert Cecil[35] on
the famine in Russia, spelling out the enormity of the problem and
suggesting forms which relief work might take, recommending among
other measures the movement of population from the Volga region, the
rebuilding of key railway lines, the granting of an amnesty to Russian
refugees now urgently needed at home, and the provision of large
credits—not to the Soviet Government, but to a 'coalition' government
which the Soviets would have to set up as the price of obtaining foreign
credit. At the same time he wrote along similar lines to Mr Berzin,[36]
chief representative of the Soviet Trade Delegation in London, stating
that he was no Communist, but asking him to transmit his views to the
Communist rulers of Russia on the need for a political amnesty, the
abolition of the Cheka, the reinstatement of Cossack self-rule, and the
formation of a central coalition government in Moscow. No doubt his
concluding appeal to the Soviets to 'enter the ways of Mercy and
Sacrifice' was received with some amusement in the capital. In April
1922 an article by him on 'The Position in Russia' appeared in the
English Review.[37] While concerned particularly with the famine and its
consequences, he spoke up in this article on behalf of the one and a half
million Russians abroad who wanted to return home and reiterated the
need to set up a coalition government, put an end to terrorism and the
confiscation of private property, recognize foreign debts, drastically
reduce the size of the Red Army, and restore Cossack self-rule in order
to win the support of the population of the fertile agricultural region of
the South. In a series of ten unpublished articles, Aladin continued his
appraisal of the Soviet situation as Russia faced the winter of 1922.[38]
Some of his observations were percipient and, had they been more
felicitously expressed, would certainly have merited publication.
Russia, he claimed, would not remain a divided country for long. It
would be wrong to count on Ukrainian separatism. Armenia and
Georgia were too small to form permanent independent states. Even
the Baltic republics would one day come into closer contact again with

[35] 21 Aug. 1921, in JRL, Box 33.
[36] 23 Aug. 1921, in JRL, Box 33.
[37] *English Review*, Apr. 1922, pp. 387–90.
[38] The set of ten articles (forty-four pages of typescript) is enclosed in a letter to DR of 6 July
1923.

Russia. The Russian peasantry were more than holding their own and producing the food for themselves and the towns, while industrial production had broken down. Russia's misfortune was not that its government was a *Soviet* government, but that it was a *Communist* Soviet government. The Soviets had come to stay and would outlive Communism. The military dictatorship of the Civil War was giving way to a political oligarchy, supported by a well-organized system of political police. The government was not composed only of adventurers and unscrupulous men, nor did it depend for its support exclusively on the army and the police. The strength of the revolutionary movement was in its genuine enthusiasm. There was no question of a restoration of the monarchy. But the Communists were tired, the country exhausted, the treasury empty. The Soviet leaders wanted political recognition by Europe as a means of obtaining loans. European statesmen would be wise to give it to them. It was, he concluded, in the interests of Russia to bring its exiles back home, but no pressure should be exerted to repatriate them against their will.

Two poorly written, but sensible articles on Constantinople and the Straits were accepted by the *Evening Standard* in October 1922,[39] the substance of them being that Russia had not the material strength to fight for the control of the Straits, that Turkey was stronger than the Bolsheviks allowed for, and that Europe should help her as a potential bulwark in the Near East. On a less realistic level was his unpublished typescript entitled 'A Practical Step in the Reconstruction of Russia',[40] with its quixotic proposal to found an organ of conciliation between Reds and Whites to be called 'Russia', to be written in Russian and published in London or Paris, which would seek to establish the truth about Russia and would be distributed both in Russia and in Russian circles abroad. There is no doubt that Aladin gave the impression at times of running with the hares and hunting with the hounds—an impression which was strengthened by his attempts to keep all possible channels open in pursuit of his overriding concern to improve relations between his native and adopted countries. In the spring of 1922, for example, he paid visits to and corresponded with officials of both the Soviet Trade Delegation and the Imperial Russian Consulate-General in London, in the former case to argue that the Soviet Government should recognize past debts and obligations, in the latter case to press for closer business ties between Britain and Russia, despite the existence of a Communist government.[41] The main thrust of Aladin's thinking about Russia in 1923 and 1924, as expressed in his private

[39] Copies dated 13 and 14 Oct. are enclosed in a letter to CN of 11 Nov. 1923.
[40] Text in JRL, Box 27.
[41] Letter to Berzin of 10 Feb. 1922, in JRL, Box 9. The visit to the Russian Consulate-General took place in May 1922.

.correspondence, was that the country was not disintegrating, and if threatened from without would speedily close ranks. Russia was, he believed, a safe country for investments and should at once be accorded diplomatic recognition by Great Britain. When this eventually happened, Aladin proudly announced that the terms of recognition were the same as those proposed by himself nearly eighteen months previously. He noted with satisfaction that early in 1924 the Bolsheviks had admitted that the peasantry were their most formidable opponents, thus confirming his own reading of the Russian economic situation. When a Soviet delegation came to London in April 1924 he offered them his assistance in their negotiations with the British, but his overtures were diplomatically rejected. He told Russell in the summer of 1924 that he saw no reason to expect any change of government in Russia in the near future; he castigated the stupidity of the Whites with the exception of Vrangel', and branded the recently deceased Lenin as 'a typical opportunist', with no deep love or hatred of anything, good or bad.[42]

Aladin's mission to Prague in the winter of 1924 and his hope of seeing a Russian Cossack and Peasant Bank established there has already been referred to. The failure of this venture was followed a year or two later by a renewed burst of journalistic writing on Russian political themes, émigré and Soviet. The main conclusions which he drew from attending the Paris Conference of Russians Abroad on behalf of the *Daily Express*[43] were that Russian émigrés, unlike French émigrés more than a century previously, had moved to countries more politically advanced than their own and had learned political wisdom. The extreme reactionary Russian ruling class was dead and the Russian aristocracy abroad had widened its political horizons. No one now believed in the liberation of Russia from outside. No one was afraid that the country would be dismembered, although fears were expressed at the conference that foreign governments might consolidate the Communist regime by lending it too much support. More on the level of wishful thinking, Aladin added that Russian industrialists abroad were beginning to look with more respect on the peasant masses as the force which would ultimately bring freedom to their native land.

Aladin received a fee for his articles, but the *Daily Express* did not publish them. Nor did the *Chicago Tribune* accept his manuscript 'Russian Communists are Feeling the Pinch',[44] in which he argued that the realization of Lenin's dream of union between industrial workers and peasants was a very long way off, since the peasants, who enjoyed a

[42] DR, letters of 16 and 17 Aug. 1924.
[43] Articles included with letters to DR in April and May 1926.
[44] The manuscript is included with a letter to DR of 24 Aug. 1926.

large numerical superiority and played a vital role in the export of grain, were, politically speaking, very doubtful allies of the Communists. In October 1926 the *Morning Post* published three articles by Aladin entitled 'Russian Communist Dissensions'[45] which briefly analysed the leading personalities of the Centre, Left, and Right factions of the Communist Party and contended that while the Centre was trying to follow the directions taken by Lenin, its policies were timid and vacillating, and open to attack from the Left in the cause of world revolution and the Right in the name of greater freedom and democracy. Aladin's pen portraits of the leaders involved are not without perceptiveness. Stalin, he said, was more feared than respected, but was obeyed unreservedly. Bukharin was undoubtedly the ablest theoretical exponent of Communism. Kalinin was essentially a figurehead, Kamenev an able, well-read journalist with a rather heavy style. Underlying the dissensions among the various groups was, he believed, the profoundly unsatisfactory condition of the country's economy and, hanging over it, the shadow of the peasant masses. The theme of dissension was taken further in 'The Split in Russia' (*Morning Post*, 16 Oct. 1926), an article written by Aladin but not attributed to him. Two reasons for the growing unrest in Russia, he rightly said, were the change in the character of the membership of the Communist Party and the split between those who wished to consolidate the national and international position of the USSR and those who regarded Russia merely as the jumping-off ground for world revolution; and he touched cautiously on a more delicate aspect of the division when he observed that nearly all the members of the ruling clique were Russians, while leaders of the opposition were predominantly Jews. Despite the presence of warring factions within the Party, Aladin believed in the essential stability of the Communist Government in Russia, a view not popular, he said, with the *Morning Post* or those British circles which looked for precedents in the French Revolution, and which may have accounted for the newspaper's rejection of two articles on the subject which correctly foresaw the outcome of the conflict between Rykov, Kalinin, and Stalin, on the one hand, and Zinov'ev and Trotsky, on the other.

In the late summer of 1926 Aladin sought and obtained a 'long and frank' interview with Bogomolov, first secretary in charge of the Soviet Embassy in London, and a man of peasant extraction.[46] Aladin wore a white carnation, which he thought befitted the occasion. In a letter confirming what had been discussed[47] Aladin spelled out his request to be provided with information on the current political and economic

---

[45] 6, 7, and 8 Oct. 1926.
[46] CN, 14 Aug. 1926.
[47] 14 Aug. 1926, in St Andrews University Library.

situation in Russia. He referred to himself as a peasant leader and emphasized his wish to strengthen his lifelong connections with the peasant movement in his country. In reply Bogomolov[48] assured him that the contents of his letter had been transmitted to Moscow and that he would do all in his power to provide the information required. Another meeting took place at the Soviet Embassy in October at which Bogomolov and the Soviet Consul General 'had their own ideas about using me'.[49] Aladin told Russell that one of the Soviet officials present seemed to assume that he wished to go back to Russia! He also told Russell that the British 'may try again what they tried in 1920–21, that is to say to press me to return to Russia'.[50] But if the question of a return, under whatever auspices, was ever seriously mooted, it was soon shelved, as Aladin's rapidly declining health confined him perforce for the rest of his life to England.

Aladin's anxious concern for what was happening in his native land did not mean that he was uninterested in the European, and especially the British, social and political scene. Despite his failure to establish himself there, he was fanatically devoted to Great Britain, its army, and many of its institutions. As a soldier himself he venerated Lord Kitchener as 'the greatest military leader Britain ever had'.[51] He religiously observed Remembrance Sunday at the Cenotaph in White-hall. He greatly admired the Dowager Queen Alexandra, even to the extent of celebrating Alexandra Day, and he felt the same love and devotion to the young Prince of Wales as the living embodiment of the Empire. He wrote affectionately of 'the red coloured areas on the map of the world',[52] and thanked God that India was part of the British Empire. To Russell he remarked that the soundest way of meeting the dangers of Communism was to make the British Empire a living reality, to organize a 'flow and reflow' of its population, and to ensure that the needs of the Empire were satisfied as far as possible by the Empire itself.[53] On the subject of British statesmen he commented that he liked Bonar Law better than any public man he knew except Lord Kitchener and Rosebery, and he had some flattering things to say about the solid, unspectacular virtues of Mr Baldwin. For Winston Churchill he predicted a glorious future. Lloyd George's political career, he believed, would be greatly enhanced by his proposed visit to Russia, and he intended to suggest that he should accompany the Liberal leader as secretary and interpreter—a plan which, like the visit itself, came to nothing. Aladin's interest in British foreign policy was largely focused on the need for, and the possibility of, better Anglo-Russian relations. As far as Britain's European neighbours were concerned, he was understandably more sympathetic to France than to

[48] 24 Aug. 1926, in JRL, Box 6.   [49] CN, 8 Oct. 1926.   [50] DR, 19 Oct. 1926.
[51] CN, 5 June 1926.   [52] CN, 16 March 1923.   [53] DR, 2 Oct. 1925.

Germany, and was critical of what he felt was Curzon's hostile attitude to the former and more lenient approach to the latter on the issue of war reparations. He remained mistrustful of Germany and feared that military elements were once again beginning to get the upper hand there. He strongly opposed the idea, supported by Germany and 'some Anglo-Saxon elements', of reviving Austria and Hungary in a new Danubian Confederation, and wished to make Czechoslovakia the leading centre of influence in the south-east corner of Central Europe.[54] Somewhat surprisingly he professed admiration for Mussolini, arguing that he was not a dictator, but a leader who had come forward at a time when the country was threatened by 'civil war of a Communist nature' and had therefore to use repressive measures which, even so, could not be remotely compared with those resorted to by the Communists in Russia and were no worse than what had happened in Turkey.[55] Underlying all Aladin's political views was the belief that under the influence of the Great War and the Russian Revolution there was a tidal wave of popular movement to the left in Europe; that Moscow was on the crest of the wave; and that the sooner 'vital connections' were established between Russia and the rest of Europe the better for the peace of the world.

Aladin's devotion to his adopted country is amply testified by the numerous references in his correspondence to his pilgrimages to London's great religious and secular monuments. Westminster Abbey was for him the spiritual heart of the British Empire. Hardly a week went by without a visit to the British Museum or one of the capital's other major museums and art galleries, and he seldom missed the Royal Academy's summer exhibitions. What is more surprising, however, is to read of this displaced Russian peasant leader's informed interest in the Derby and the St Leger, or the fact that he wore a light blue favour on Boat Race Day.

The *Manchester Guardian*'s obitary notice called Aladin 'a sad man, but one singularly without bitterness'.[56] His uncomplaining acceptance of innumerable rebuffs (for all his militant instincts) and the spiritual calm which he maintained in the face of personal and private tragedies was due in no small measure to his deep religious faith. Aladin had a conventional Christian upbringing in the Russian Orthodox Church, and after a youthful period of indifference to organized religion, became more and more preoccupied as he grew older with the life of the spirit. He was intimately acquainted with the Bible, and read the New Testament in Greek. He was profoundly interested in all aspects of mysticism, and on the subject of spiritualism he claimed to

[54] DR, 11 Jan. 1925.
[55] Letters to DR (13 Nov. 1926) and CN (22 Nov. 1926).
[56] *Manchester Guardian*, 6 Aug. 1927.

have read everything worth reading. His acceptance of Christianity, albeit on his own terms, did not diminish his interest in the scriptures of the great religions of India and China, references to and quotations from which, together with recommended reading, frequently occur in his correspondence. It was, however, the religion of the ancient pharaohs which held a peculiar fascination for him and prompted a series of unpublished articles on 'The Living Soul of Ancient Egypt'[57] (correctly described by himself as 'rugged and uncouth'), and one published article of more merit: 'Ikhnaton and Bolshevism'.[58] Drawing heavily on Breasted,[59] Aladin offered an interpretation of the short reign of Amenhotep IV which he believed provided an instructive analogy with the early days of the Bolshevik regime. On assuming the role of High Priest, Amenhotep began his task of transforming the established religion of his people, in the course of which a new ceremonial had to be created, new hymns written, new music composed, new temples built, a new priesthood constituted, and all opposition to the old creed overcome. The new religion, allegedly, was the product of 'the reasoning mind', and lacked the qualities of love and mercy. Its High Priest assumed a new name (Ikhnaton) and moved his capital from Thebes to another part of Egypt. A bitter struggle followed, the court and administration became servile, and enemies encroached upon the land. Parallels with the Bolshevik revolution in its infancy, Aladin argued, could easily be drawn; and if the analogy is flawed by the paucity and conflicting nature of the evidence concerning Amenhotep's reign, it is an interesting illustration of the originality of Aladin's mind as well as the unusually broad range of his historical and religious interests.

If Aladin's overriding intellectual interest was in mysticism and religion, he was at the same time an assiduous armchair student of the physical sciences. Trained as a scientist at Kazan' University, where he achieved distinction in a number of subjects before being expelled, he spent much time on his return to England in the Science Museum at Kensington, closely followed the proceedings of the British Association, and tried to keep abreast of the latest developments in physics in the Reading Room of the British Museum. If there was one scientific field in which he could claim expertise it was aeronautics. Before the war, he said, he had made his name in Russia as a special aviation correspondent for *Novoe Vremya*, writing under the *nom de plume* of 'Rover'. During the war he was given the opportunity both in England and France to study and comment on the development of military aircraft. Back in Britain he was a regular attender at Hendon air

---

[57] The articles are enclosed in a letter to CN of 31 May 1923.
[58] *The Quest*, Apr. 1923, pp. 377–88.
[59] J. H. Breasted, *A History of Egypt* (London, 1921).

displays and once boasted to an Air Ministry official that he had been 'connected with British aviation from its infancy'.[60] To his great disappointment, however, his considerable technical knowledge and his engineering experience acquired in pre-war Southampton were never put to use in post-war London.

Like his mother, Aladin was undoubtedly more than a little 'fey'. Highly imaginative and intuitive and seemingly gifted with hypnotic prophetic powers, he was conscious of being different from his fellow men. A romantic by nature, he loved to read fairy-tales, especially Russian tales, a number of which he translated and passed on to Miss Nightingale 'to touch with the magic wand of English'.[61] His favourite authors included, in English, Kipling and R. L. Stevenson, in Russian Korolenko (especially *Makar's Dream* and *Shades*), and, among classical writers, Apuleius, whose *Golden Ass* he re-read many times. He was acutely receptive to the beauties of nature and was passionately fond of flowers, which he could never bear to be without even in times of direst poverty. Yet together with an abnormally heightened sensitivity went an aggressive streak, a pugnacity which showed through even in the military metaphors he was wont to use. He liked to think of himself as a fighter, and in his pantheon of heroes Lord Kitchener occupied a place not much lower than Jesus Christ. If his loyalty to Britain was great, his pride in being Russian was even greater. When Dean Inge in an article in the *Evening Standard* entitled 'New Russia: What it means' warned his countrymen against 'the inferior race of the Slavs' and branded the Russians as 'half Tartars', Aladin wrote an angry letter to the editor, who refused to publish it, which put an end to his own relations with the paper.[62] To Miss Nightingale he wrote: 'East is East and West is West, and they meet in Russia.'[63] Russia could bridge the gap, he thought, because she combined the energy of Norsemen, Greeks, and Tatars with the contemplative powers of the Slavs. Energy and the faculty of contemplation were certainly much in evidence in Aladin's make-up. So too was pride. Immensely gifted, and not unaware of it, he seemed genuinely puzzled when English friends advised him 'to become more humble'. Politician, journalist, engineer, soldier, religious philosopher—he might have excelled in any one of many fields. In the event he ended his days in lonely obscurity, dependent on charity to pay the rent. From the Tauride Palace in St Petersburg to a bed-sitter in Hampstead was an odyssey which even he, with his self-proclaimed powers of second sight, could not have predicted.

[60] CN, 15 June 1925.
[61] CN 24 Nov. 1922.
[62] Aladin's letter of 27 Oct. 1922 in reply to Dean Inge's article of Oct. 1922 is in JRL, Box 9.
[63] CN, 8 July 1921.